IN SEARCH OF BISCO

ERSKINE CALDWELL

IN SEARCH
OF BISCO

Foreword by Wayne Mixon

Brown Thrasher Books

THE UNIVERSITY OF GEORGIA PRESS

Athens and London

Published in 1995 as a Brown Thrasher Book
by the University of Georgia Press, Athens, Georgia 30602
© 1965, 1993 by Erskine Caldwell
Foreword to the Brown Thrasher Edition © 1995
by the University of Georgia Press

The paper in this book meets the guidelines for
permanence and durability of the Committee on
Production Guidelines for Book Longevity of the
Council on Library Resources.

Printed in the United States of America

99   98   97   96   95   P   5   4   3   2   1

Library of Congress Cataloging in Publication Data

Caldwell, Erskine, 1903–
In search of Bisco / Erskine Caldwell; foreword by Wayne Mixon
p.   cm.
Originally published: New York : Farrar, Straus and Giroux,
1965.
"Brown thrasher books."
Includes bibliographical references.
ISBN 0-8203-1784-5 (pbk. : alk. paper)
1. Caldwell, Erskine, 1903–   —Homes and haunts—Southern
States.   2. Caldwell, Erskine, 1903–   —Childhood and
youth.   3. Novelists, American—20th century—Biography.
4. Afro-Americans—Southern States.   5. Southern States—
Race relations.   I. Title.
PS3505.A322Z466   1995
813'.52—dc20
[B]   95-14565

British Library Cataloging in Publication Data available

Foreword

Wayne Mixon

In Search of Bisco was published in the spring of
1965, coincidentally at a crucial time in the civil rights
movement. The Selma March had occurred not long
before, and the passage of the Voting Rights Act would
occur not long after. Perhaps those circumstances generated a high degree of interest in Erskine Caldwell's
book among southerners, many of whom had given
little notice to his works of the previous decade.

Whatever caused the attention accorded *In Search
of Bisco*, the book was reviewed widely in the South.
Many reviewers were hostile, branding Caldwell a
"fire-breathing liberal" who reported "no news but bad
news and no South but a bad South" and who offered
"nothing new in this one-sided slap at dear old Dixie."
But many other reviewers were friendly, describing
In Search of Bisco as "thoughtful and thought-

provoking," "eloquent and painful," "strong . . . [and] moving." The highest praise came from Frank Daniel of the *Atlanta Journal*, Caldwell's friend who had known him ever since he worked briefly for the newspaper forty years before. Daniel reminded readers of the *Journal* that Caldwell had been fighting racial injustice for all of those forty years. "Few writers," Daniel observed, "have the authority and the power to speak now as he can here."[1] Daniel was right. Among white southern writers of Caldwell's generation, none fought the evil of racism for as long and in so forthright a manner as Caldwell.

Had Caldwell not been raised by parents who wanted to make the world a better place, he probably would not have acquired his keen awareness of social injustice. His mother, Caroline Bell Caldwell, was a schoolteacher and a writer of columns for a religious journal. In her classroom, where she taught Latin and English, Mrs. Caldwell emphasized the importance of liberal education. In her columns, she demonstrated sympathy for down-and-out people, white and black, and called for the improvement of their conditions. Erskine's father, the Reverend Ira Sylvester Caldwell, an ardent advocate of the social gospel within the archly conservative Associate Reformed Presbyterian Church, served the cause of social reform throughout his career. Among the great evils of the Reverend Caldwell's place and time—the American South early in the twentieth century—were poverty and racial oppression. Caldwell's father battled those enemies of the good society from the pulpit, in the classroom, and on the printed page. His fight often aroused opposition from other white southerners, including Ku Klux Klansmen who branded him a "nigger lover."

Erskine was also fortunate to have a father who gave him free rein to explore the world around him. Moreover, his father's work—be it as regular pastor or as supply preacher—required that the family move often. Growing up, Erskine lived in Georgia, the Carolinas, Virginia, Florida, and Tennessee. As a result of the family's frequent moves and his father's tolerance of youthful inquisitiveness, Caldwell amassed a wealth of experiences and observations that would later enrich his writing.

Of all the early influences, the strongest by far was that of his father. Like Ira Caldwell, Erskine was enraged by economic injustice in the South. He displayed that rage in *Tobacco Road, God's Little Acre, You Have Seen Their Faces,* and other works that are not as well known as those books of the 1930s. Like Ira, Erskine was also enraged by racial injustice in the South. He exhibited that rage throughout his sixty year career. By and large, his fight against racism has been unacknowledged for many years.

At the outset of his career, Caldwell showed a sensitivity to racial inequities that was extraordinary for a white southerner in the 1920s. As a reporter for the *Atlanta Journal* and simultaneously a book reviewer for a syndicate based at the *Charlotte Observer,* he was introduced to scholarly works that dealt with the lives and culture of black Americans. Those books left a deep impression. He believed that Newbell Niles Puckett's *Folk Beliefs of the Southern Negro* should command the attention of all white southerners who desired improvement in race relations. Regarding Jerome Dowd's *The Negro in American Life*, he wrote: "No one who is interested in the advancement of society can afford to be without . . . [this] book."[2] In another early publication, an essay written when he was a student at the University of Virginia following his stint with the *Journal*, he attacked the oppression of blacks as one of the many ills that plagued his native Georgia.

During the 1930s and into the 1940s, as his work became known in America and throughout the world, Caldwell's assault on racism grew ever more relentless. In short story after short story—for example, "Saturday Afternoon," "Candy-Man Beechum," "Kneel to the Rising Sun," and "The End of Christy Tucker"— he exposed the iniquity of a system that allowed white southerners to kill black men for being good at their work, for speaking out against mistreatment, or for merely being big and strong. The stories depicting racial injustice, told with great skill and possessing overwhelming power, are the best works that Caldwell produced. At the beginning of the 1940s, Caldwell used race for the first time as the central theme of a novel. *Trouble in July*, a compelling tale about the lynching of an innocent black youth, was clearly intended to serve the cause of the antilynching movement that had emerged in the South.

Much of Caldwell's nonfiction of the thirties and early forties also attacked racism. His reports of racial unrest in a Georgia town near his parents' home, filed at great personal risk, brought national attention to the killing of three black men. Without his exposé, those slayings would have received little notice. His travel writing, another genre in which he excelled, dealt often with the discrimination suffered by blacks in the South. *Some American People*, *You Have Seen Their Faces*, and *Say, Is This the U.S.A.* contain segments that blast the racism of white southerners. *You Have Seen Their Faces* and *Say, Is This the U.S.A.* were illustrated with pictures taken by Margaret Bourke-White, an esteemed photographer who was Caldwell's wife for three years. Her photographs authenticated his anger.

Caldwell's attacks on racial injustice occasionally received the endorsement of his fellow southerners. In 1931, Aaron Blum Bernd, a white reviewer in Macon, Georgia, lauded his condemnation of lynching; nine years later, a black reviewer, the Mississippi writer Richard Wright, also praised his assault on the barbaric practice. Usually, though, southern commentators reacted defensively to his portrayal of lynching, as they excoriated his treatment of race generally. Sometimes, they vilified him as well; responding to *Trouble in July*, a Georgian called him "the personification of an earthworm."[3] Even such an enlightened southerner as William Terry Couch, the director of the University of North Carolina Press and a leading figure in the South's intellectual awakening, condemned Caldwell for what Couch considered to be irresponsible views on the race issue. The Chapel Hill liberal could not countenance Caldwell's advocacy of assimilation.

The quality of much of Caldwell's postwar fiction is far below that of most of his earlier work, the result of his waning powers as a creative writer and of his cranking out a novel annually for many years, something that he had not done before. Yet if many of the novels written after 1945 embarrass the great fiction of the 1930s, virtually all demonstrate his ongoing opposition to social injustice. Among the best of the later novels and among the most socially significant of all of Caldwell's works is *Place Called Estherville*. Published in 1949, the novel scathingly denounces the abuse of blacks and prophesies significant changes in race relations in the South. A white reviewer in Georgia expressed outrage over Caldwell's refusal to recognize that "the Negro question is not to be trifled with."[4]

Other white southerners shared that sentiment. A correspondent from New Orleans called Caldwell a "Negro loving Bas[tard]." A Georgia businessman described him as a traitor who planted "the seeds of racial hatreds to grow into the oaks of Communism." A Florida journalist, denouncing his "planned calumniation of the South," labeled him a tool of race-mixing Communists.[5]

Caldwell expected such reactions from white southerners, but he must have been surprised by a letter that he received from a Georgian who described himself as "a full-blooded Negro." The correspondent, angry over Caldwell's depiction of miscegenation, called him "a dirty, lying son-of-a-bitch."[6]

Refusing to be intimidated by racist southerners, black or white, Caldwell continued to address the issue of racial hatred. Many of his novels of the 1960s display his sympathy for people who are social outcasts because they are black, and one novel scores blacks who reject someone because he is white.

In the later part of his career, however, Caldwell would present his most forceful treatment of race in nonfiction rather than in fiction. Early in the 1960s, his new publisher, Farrar, Straus and Cudahy, suggested that he write three works of nonfiction over the course of the decade. Recognizing Caldwell's strengths, the firm wanted a description of folkways in the United States, an examination of evangelical religion in the South, and a portrayal of race relations in Dixie.

In fulfilling his publisher's assignments, Caldwell gathered information just as he had in the thirties and forties. He conducted research not by reading books or newspapers but on the road, by talking to people. Furthermore, he used the same technique to refine data that he had developed thirty years before: after making notes of conversations or observations, he would, as he described the method, "reconstitute— not recreate but reconstitute—the atmosphere, the tenor" of what he had heard or seen.[7]

Although Caldwell was in his sixties when he wrote

the travel books of the 1960s, he did not let age impede his efforts. He worked diligently on the books. He and his wife, Virginia, who accompanied him on the journeys, developed a routine. Each day they would rise before dawn, travel and collect information until late afternoon, and then find new lodging. At that point, Caldwell would begin to write. Caldwell was deeply dedicated to his work. While working on one project, he suffered from an ailing hand. He relieved the pain by hoisting the hand to the ceiling of his motel room. With his good hand, he pecked away at his typewriter.

In 1963, Erskine and Virginia journeyed across the country gathering material that appeared the following year in *Around About America*. The parts of the book—a fourth of its contents—that deal with the South depict, among other matters, poverty in Appalachia and the viciously racist acts of some white southerners. Caldwell also deplored the Confederate flags flying over government buildings because such displays gave official sanction to the denigration of black southerners. If white southerners wanted to celebrate a symbol of rebellion, Caldwell felt, they should do so in museums.

In 1968, four years after the publication of *Around About America*, Caldwell's examination of evangelical religion appeared in a volume entitled *Deep South*. As he condemned both the fanatical fundamentalism of members of rural white churches and the complacent conservatism of members of urban white

churches, he lauded the social activism of black southern evangelicals who led the civil rights movement.

In 1964, the year in which Caldwell and his wife
traveled the South to gather material for *In Search of
Bisco*, he wrote to Martin Luther King Jr. to congratu-
late him for being awarded the Nobel Peace Prize and
to say: "I am proud to be one of your fellow citizens."[8]
During their trip, which Caldwell's ninety-two-year-
old mother urged them not to take because she feared
for their safety, Erskine and Virginia suffered some of
the mistreatment familiar to civil rights workers. Both
of them were vilified as outside agitators, and on an
occasion when Virginia was not in her husband's presence, she was harassed by police.

What Caldwell discovered on his journey from
South Carolina to Louisiana looking for Bisco, a black
playmate of his early childhood, dampened the op-
timistic prediction of improvement in race relations
that he expressed the year before. In *Around About
America*, he had written that the efforts of blacks who
were aware that they were "entitled to full citizenship" would make "equal rights and racial freedom" a reality within fifteen years.[9] Most of the whites
that Caldwell encountered in his search for Bisco had
no intention of allowing blacks to gain equal rights and
racial freedom. Those whites were often people of
social prominence—not stereotypical racists—who
sometimes expressed their opposition to the civil
rights movement viciously and obscenely. As for the
blacks with whom Caldwell spoke, some had good

reason to hate whites. None, however, displayed the racist sentiments of many of the whites he met. What the blacks wanted was the chance to achieve economic security.

Yet, as Caldwell learned in his search for Bisco, some blacks had no reason to hope for betterment of their condition. The twin evils of racism and poverty flourished in the South of his old age just as they had in the South of his youth. Caldwell never quit fighting injustice because he had learned well the lessons that his father had taught him: have compassion for the less fortunate, work to improve their situation, and never judge someone by the color of his skin. A profoundly moral writer, Caldwell battled social injustice with all of his might for all of his life.

NOTES

1. *Charleston News and Courier*, 18 April 1965; *Austin American-Statesman*, 11 April 1965; *Pensacola News Journal*, 9 May 1965; *Nashville Banner*, 30 April 1965; *Norfolk Pilot*, 11 April 1965; *Rocky Mount Telegram*, 18 April 1965; *Atlanta Journal*, 11 April 1965, Erskine Caldwell Collection, Dartmouth College Library.

2. Erskine Caldwell, review of *The Negro in American Life*, by Jerome Dowd, *Charlotte Observer*, 21 November 1926.

3. *Gainesville News*, 20 March 1940, Erskine Caldwell Collection, Dartmouth College Library.

4. *Augusta Herald*, 29 September 1949, *Scrapbooks of*

Erskine Caldwell (microfilm ed.; Ann Arbor, 1974), reel four.

5. Larry W. King to Erskine Caldwell, 28 February 1954, Erskine Caldwell Collection, Dartmouth College Library; *Albany Herald*, 16 June 1948, *Scrapbooks of Erskine Caldwell*, reel four; *Jacksonville Times-Union*, 31 October 1959, *Scrapbooks of Erskine Caldwell*, reel five.

6. "An American" to Erskine Caldwell, 9 March 1952, Erskine Caldwell Collection, Dartmouth College Library.

7. Quoted in Harvey L. Klevar, *Erskine Caldwell: A Biography* (Knoxville, 1993), 151–52.

8. Ibid., 377.

9. Erskine Caldwell, *Around About America* (New York, 1964), 55.

IN SEARCH OF BISCO

1

The scene of my first becoming aware of the existence of color differences among people was my birthplace on an isolated farm deep in the piney-wood country of the red clay hills of Coweta County in Middle Georgia. My introduction to the reality of a dividing line between white-skin people and black-skin people was abrupt.

The time remembered in the beginning was during the first decade of the century when I was five-years-old-going-on-six. My only playmate was a Negro boy called Bisco whose father was a tall, lean, one-mule sharecropper on the adjoining cotton farm and whose mother was a huge soft-fleshed woman who had often let both of us sit on her lap at the same time while she sang mournful songs to us.

My playmate's given name may have been Nabisco

or Frisco or Brisco, but to me he was Bisco and he called me Esk. We were within a few weeks of being the same age and neither of us had brothers or sisters for playmates.

Bisco had close-cropped kinky black hair, mulatto-colored skin, a chubby round face, an open-mouth grin, and he went barefooted in summer and winter. Whenever we played rough-and-tumble and wrestled on the ground, cockleburs and sawdust and weed-fluff clung to his hair. He had a habit of suddenly calling quits and stopping our playing rough-and-tumble once in a while to stand up and brush the burs and chaff from his head with quick flailing motions of his hands. After that Bisco would get down on the ground again and wrestle some more.

On this particular day, now so long ago, after a morning of wrestling, Bisco and I had been playing with our hand-whittled wooden boats through an autumn afternoon in the smooth white sand under my mother and father's high-pillared, four-room, breezeway house. Night came early in late autumn in Middle Georgia and there was a chilly dampness in the gusty wind.

Bisco began to shiver all over as soon as the sun went down and, flailing the sand and sawdust from his hair, he said he was going home. I begged him to stay and play just a little while longer, but he said he was cold and wanted to go home where it would be warm by the fireplace. He lived with his mother and father in a one-room-and-kitchen-lean-to cabin in the middle of a cotton patch no more than a quarter of a mile away. I could see the blue smoke of a pitch-pine fire coming from the chimney of the clay-chinked log cabin, and there was a good smell of pine smoke coming all the way to my house.

His teeth chattering with cold, Bisco picked up his boats and started down the path through the tall blackberry thicket in the twilight. He looked backward at me several times without saying a word and, just before he started through the thicket, I ran to catch up with him.

I had often gone to Bisco's house to play in his yard, but always in the daytime and never after dark, and this time I wanted so much to keep on playing with him that I had no thought of asking my parents if I could go home with him.

Both of us were shivering with cold when we got to the cabin and Bisco's mother told us to stand on the brick hearth and warm ourselves in front of the flaming pine-log fire. It was Bisco's suppertime, and his mother brought both of us plates of pan-fried pork chops and helpings of chitterling bread and large tin cups of hot collard pot-likker. We sat down in front of the roaring fire and ate from the plates on the hearth.

As soon as we had finished eating, Bisco's mother undressed him and put him into the big high-posted bed and covered him with colorful cotton patch-work quilts. While she was tucking him in bed, I took off my shirt and pants and tried to get under the covers with him.

Gently, but firmly, his mother took me by the hand and made me stand in front of the fireplace while she dressed me. During all that time I was begging her to let me stay and get into bed with Bisco, but she was shaking her head and telling me that my mother wanted me to come home and sleep in my own bed. Pleading and begging and tears had no effect at all, and I was taken by her warm hand and led down the path through the cotton patch in the darkness toward the blackberry thicket and my own home.

Just as we were entering the path through the thicket, we saw my father coming toward us with a lantern in his hand. In the dim light he appeared to be neither surprised nor angry when he reached for me to take me home, but I could see him shaking his head in the lantern light when I began begging him to let me go back and spend the night with Bisco under the thick warm quilts.

I began to cry when I had to release my grip on the Negro woman's warm hand, but my father picked me up and, holding the lantern in his other hand, we went along the thicket path to our house. I stopped crying then and put my arms around my father's neck to keep warm in the cold night. As we went toward home in the lantern light, he was saying that my mother wanted me to sleep in my own bed so she would know where I was and that Bisco's mother wanted him to sleep in his own bed so she could watch over him and not be worried about his being away from home after dark.

Just before reaching our house, I saw my mother waiting for us in the lighted doorway and my father put me down and I ran to the porch. When I begged her to let me spend the next night with Bisco, she said that it was time to put a stop to anything like that and that I was never to go to his house again. When I asked her why, she said that it was because I was white and he was Negro, and that I was old enough to learn that we had to live in separate houses.

Thinking then only of the blazing pine-log fire and the big quilt-covered bed in Bisco's house, I was still unhappy about having been brought home. But even when I told my mother that Bisco always had fried pork chops and chitterling bread and collard pot-likker for supper, she was still unrelenting. However, she said that if I would promise never to go to his house again, I could have the same things for supper sometime. It took me a long time to make a promise like that because Bisco was my friend and I was still unhappy about it even when she said I could put my plate on the hearth in front of the fireplace and eat supper exactly like Bisco did in his house.

All that took place a long time ago in years. Nevertheless, in both time and implication, the recollection of it has continued to remain clear and meaningful and unchanging.

The scene of my next recollection of Negro life in the United States was near the Mississippi River on a country road in the soft, dark, rain-damp soil of Tipton County in West Tennessee. I was about fourteen years old at the time and in the eighth grade of school.

I was walking alone along the muddy road from school one afternoon in September when, midway of the three miles from school to home, I saw a group of about a dozen white farmers and timber cutters talking excitedly in front of the grocery store at the crossroads. It was about four o'clock in the afternoon and the heat of summer was still clinging to the earth. The men were dressed, as they usually were at that time of the week, in mud-stained bibbed overalls and were wearing sun-browned field-straw hats. I sat down on the weedy bank of the drain ditch on the far side of the dirt road and wondered what the gesturing, loud-talking, tobacco-chewing men were talking about so excitedly.

It was not unusual to see that many white farmers and timber cutters at the crossroads store on Saturday afternoons, and at such a time ordinarily there would have been as many Negro men talking among themselves in a separate group nearby. However, it was then the middle of the week and there was no Negro within sight.

I had been sitting on the ditch bank for about a quarter of an hour, too far away to be able to hear what was being said, and by then I was curious to find out what had happened that was the cause of so much excitement. Usually, such a group of farmers and timbermen would have laughed from time to time and there would have been a few intervals of silence. But this time several men were talking at once and nobody had laughed. I crossed the road and went close enough to the men to be able to hear what was being said.

A schoolboy among men in those years knew better than to ask a prying question or to interrupt adult conversation at a country store without specific invitation. Otherwise, if he had made such a mistake, it was likely that he would get a box on the ears or a splatter of tobacco juice in the eyes.

So many men were talking, and doing so without the usual vagueness of casual conversation, that it was not long until I had put enough together to learn that a young Negro boy named Sonny Brown had been accused of raping a twenty-year-old white girl on a farm two miles away. Early in the morning of that same day, as I heard it, Sonny, instead of going into hiding or running away, had gone to work as usual at the lumber mill where he had a job shoveling sawdust. The father of the girl, a brother, and several other men had gone to the lumber mill, strung Sonny from the limb of a tree, and blasted his life away with shotguns.

I had never seen the girl they were talking about, but I had heard some of the older boys at school tell how easy it was for anybody to buy a sack of sugar-coated gumdrops or chocolate candy and go for a walk in the woods with her and watch her strip naked. The older boys said she always begged for intercourse after getting naked and eating the candy. I had seen Sonny nearly every time I went to the crossroads store on Saturday afternoons and he and I had gone fishing together in Blue Creek twice that summer.

While I had been listening, the arguments among the men had become tense and voices were loud. Some of the men were saying they were sure that the girl, who had been a known prostitute for several years, had deliberately lied about being raped and that Sonny should not have been lynched. Others were saying that no Negro who had had sexual intercourse with a white girl, even a whore, ought to be allowed to stay alive. Angry threats were being made and some of the men were ready to fight.

I knew it was no place for a schoolboy at a time like that, because somebody might take out a pistol and begin shooting. I backed away from the crowd and went down the road toward home. There were frequent rumors of lynchings along the Mississippi River, as well as occasional newspaper reports of them, and such happenings were not unusual in the hot months of summer and early autumn.

However, for a long time afterward I wondered how a Negro boy anywhere would have a chance to prove, before he was lynched, that he was not guilty of raping a white girl who enticed teen-age boys of both races to give her some candy in exchange for sexual intercourse.

West Tennessee was far from Middle Georgia, but I could not keep from wondering if what had happened to Sonny would ever happen to Bisco.

The next scene of a vivid recollection of Negro life in the South was in the sand-clay level lands just below the fall line of the Piedmont Plateau in Jefferson County of East Georgia. I was about sixteen years old then and it was during the time when I spent Sunday afternoons all summer long at a chain-gang stockade where forty or more Negro convicts were shackled, balled, and chained.

The convicts, uniformly dressed in black-and-white striped pants and shirts, worked six days of the week on county roads from sunup to sundown. They were fed a pot of stew and a wedge of corn pone three times a day and, shackled with ball-and-chain leg-irons around the clock, were locked in six-foot-long movable iron cages during the hours of darkness. Their only relative freedom, though still never without ball-and-chain, was during their one day of rest on Sunday.

Wives, children, and other Negroes were never permitted to enter the stockade at any time. However, as though the convicts were being given the privilege of being on exhibition, the guards had no objection to any white person entering the compound on Sunday and staying until the prisoners were locked in their cages at sundown.

I began going to the stockade on Sunday afternoons, not because of curiosity, but because I knew one of the Negroes. His name was Roy and he had been a yardboy for a neighbor in our part of town since he was fifteen years old. When he was sixteen, he had been accused of stealing a heavy iron washpot from the backyard where he worked. Even though such a pot was too heavy for any one man to lift, and it had not been sold for scrap iron at the junk-yard, Roy had been convicted of theft and sentenced to two years at hard labor on the county chain gang.

I was sure that Roy had not taken the iron washpot, not only because it was too heavy for a man to carry, but because he told me he had not taken it. I had known him for more than a year before he was sentenced to the chain gang and I was certain he was telling the truth.

Just the same, Roy was on the chain gang and there was no likelihood of his being released until he had served the two-year term. I began going to see him at work camp on Sunday afternoons and he shined my shoes and I would ask him what he wanted that I could get for him. Ever since I had seen Roy the first time, he had reminded me of Bisco. I had no idea what Bisco would actually look like at the age of sixteen, but the three of us were the same age, and I remembered Bisco being mulatto-colored, just as Roy was, and both of them had the same open-mouth grin and friendly squint of the eyes. It was almost like being with Bisco when I went to see Roy.

The price of a shoe shine in the stockade was five cents. This was the only money a convict was permitted to earn and he had to pay for shoe polish from his earnings. Since there were forty or more Negroes on the chain gang, and rarely more than a dozen white visitors on a Sunday, it was not often that many of them could earn as much as a nickel.

At first, each time I gave Roy a nickel for a shine he would hand it back and ask me to bring him a sack of makings—flaked tobacco and cigarette papers. I soon got into the habit of taking the makings with me on Sundays and giving them to Roy as soon as I got there. Never failing to thank me, he would then roll a cigarette and puff slowly with a grateful squinting of his eyes. After that, he would spend the next hour polishing and shining my shoes while we talked about everything we could think of.

Sometimes Roy and I talked about baseball and hunting and fishing, at other times it would be about a murder or a fire or an accident that had happened to somebody in town. The convicts on the chain gang were always making up jokes and Roy would tell me all the new ones he had heard. Some of the convicts around us would usually play-the-dozens, which was a continuous sing-song festival of improvised lyrics extolling sexual aberrations and yearnings, but Roy always said that kind of talk was too vulgar for him and that he did not want to have anything to do with it. He never failed to ask me before the day was over if I knew how his mother was and if I had seen any of his brothers and sisters. And then finally, when I was leaving the stockade, I would ask Roy what else besides makings he would like for me to bring him the next time I came.

As though he felt he would be asking too much of a favor, he would say that if he ever earned a dime on Sunday he would be able to pay for two sacks of makings and have enough tobacco to last a whole week. I was soon bringing him two sacks of makings and a can of shoe polish when he needed it.

Toward the end of summer, a little more than a week before the work camp was to be moved about fifteen miles to another part of the county, I asked Roy to tell me just one other thing he would like to have most of all. Without hesitation, and as though he had been thinking about it for a long time, he said other than makings what he wanted most of all were some of the biggest fried pork chops that ever grew on a hog.

The chain-gang guards permitted no packages or bundles of any kind, other than tobacco and shoe polish, to be brought into the stockade, and everyone who entered on Sunday afternoon was searched for a file or pistol at the gate. However, I was confident that I would be able to smuggle pork chops to Roy by putting them inside my shirt and holding my arms tightly against them. I cooked four of them at home the next Sunday morning, wrapped each one in a piece of newspaper, and placed them inside my shirt.

The usual guard was not on duty at the stockade that afternoon and a younger guard I had never seen before stopped me at the gate and told me to hold my arms above my head while he searched me for hacksaw and pistol. When I raised my arms, he looked at me with a knowing grin on his face while he was feeling the pork chops. The first thing he said was that the next time I ought to wrap pork chops in a different kind of paper so the grease would not ooze through my shirt the way it did. Then, as I was going through the stockade gate, he told me that if I did it again I was going to get the reputation around town of being a nigger-lover.

I asked Roy while he was eating the pork chops if he had ever known a colored boy named Bisco. Shaking his head, he said that was a new name to him, but that it sounded good and friendly. I told him about Bisco when we were playmates and said that he and Bisco were enough alike to be brothers.

Presently, Roy looked up and said that a colored boy with a name like that ought to be a mighty fine fellow and that he hoped nobody named Bisco would ever be wrongly accused of doing something against the law and be sentenced to the chain gang or shot down by a white man's gun. Remembering what had happened to Sonny in Tennessee, and seeing the ball-and-chain shackled to Roy's legs, I told him that I hoped so, too.

2

The southside of the United States is the geographically welded region of South Carolina, Georgia, Alabama, Mississippi, Arkansas, and Louisiana. It is also a state of mind—a local purgatory or an earthly paradise—and often an economic iniquity, a social anachronism, a political autocracy, and a racial tyranny.

After placing the bordering states of Virgina, North Carolina, Kentucky, and Tennessee where they should have been relegated by a more realistic Mason and Dixon line in the beginning—which would still be north of the feudal Southerner's horizon—the domain from South Carolina to Louisiana is the authentic Deep South of fact and fiction.

But, above all, this is Bisco Country. After a lifetime of being a Negro American, Bisco is probably as familiar with its joys and sorrows as anyone else and going in search of him through the Deep South has the prospect of seeing Bisco's native land as he himself knows it.

This region of fertile fields and flourishing factories has the appearance of being a pleasant segment of America far removed and remote from the social and economic ills elsewhere in the United States. Life is relaxed and unhurried. The climate is mild and the scenery is often spectacular. People are friendly and tax collectors are apologetic.

All would be well in this land of apparent ease and pleasantry if there were only one Southerner to claim inheritance of this bountiful goodness of earth. But there is another Southerner with a rightful claim to his share of inheritance so well and deservedly earned after more than two hundred years of sweat, travail, hardship, and degredation. An equitable sharing of the reward is long past due.

The unrewarded Southerner is the Negro. After this long period of slavery, servitude, injustice, and discrimination, the Negro of the South has finally dared to speak for the past due accounting. But easily incurred debts are always the last to be repaid, and the white Protestant Southerner of Anglo-Saxon origin, resisting to the end, continues to postpone settlement by promising payment in economic opportunity and democratic citizenship in the sweet by-and-by of tomorrow and tomorrow and tomorrow.

The practice of devising methods for preventing a Negro from working in a trade or occupation or profession for which he qualifies is default by design and not by oversight. The long-standing promise of payment remains unfulfilled. It may never be said in so many words, but the implication is obvious. He is a Negro. To hell with him.

The forty-five-year-old truck driver lives in an aging hovel of weather-cracked boards and shingles on a water-puddle dirt street in the South Carolina sand hill town of Kershaw. The sand hill country has never been productive of much other than yellow sedge and scrub pines, but people live there because they were born there and it is a place to call home. It is a state-long belt of sandy land at the fall line of the Piedmont Plateau of the Appalachian and Blue Ridge mountains, rarely more than fifty miles in width, that has impoverished many generations of people long before the nineteen-sixties.

The Negro truck driver has a job washing and greasing automobiles at a gasoline station on Fridays and Saturdays. It is the only job he has been able to get, and he sits at home five days of the week hoping that someday he will be able to get a full-time truck driving job. He goes to the loading dock of the long-distance trucking company as often as he dares, being careful not to annoy the white superintendent by going too frequently, and asks when there might be a chance for him to go to work for the company. Not now, he is always told, but maybe someday. And now is the time when he is becoming fearful that he will be too old to drive a truck by the time the company finally will hire a Negro for long-distance driving.

He has a recent newspaper with a want-ad set in bold type. He looks at it and shakes his head. QUALI-FIED DRIVERS WANTED IMMEDIATELY BY LONG-DISTANCE TRUCKING COMPANY. GOOD PAY AND ALL BENEFITS. MEALS WHEN AWAY FROM HOME. FULL-TIME WORK AND NO LAY-OFFS.

If I didn't know better by now, he said, I'd be up there banging on the door instead of sitting here. They don't say white and they don't say black and they don't say nothing about color, but everybody knows what they mean. It takes a white skin to sat-isfy the company. You can have a clean driver's license and a white doctor swearing you're as healthy as a buck rabbit in a clover patch and be able to jack a twenty-wheel tractor-trailer rig in a nine-foot-wide loading dock with six inches to spare on both sides, and they still won't hire you if you're black like me.

They wanted me in the army when I was about twenty years old and I went in there just a little while after the war started the last time. The army put me through engine overhauling at first, then on the grease racks for a while, and after about six months I was running pick-up trucks around the camp. That wasn't much to brag about, but then came the best part of all. They gave me a big ten-ton refrigerator rig to make a hundred-and-forty-mile round-trip high-way run for the commissary every night. Man, that's what I call living in the Promised Land.

That's what I did in the army for just about two years and then when the war was finished they couldn't get me out of that tractor cab. What I did was turn right around and join up for four more years just so I could keep on driving the big rigs. And I sure did keep those big engines humming like brand-new sewing machines and never once let a speck of paint get scratched all that time. I was the proudest man in that whole camp.

By the time I finally left the army and came back home, I could take down a truck engine, diesel or gasoline, and put it back together with my eyes shut. That's what the army taught me about engines and I can still do it as good as any driver rolling a truck on the highway. Knowing how your engine ought to hum and how the exhaust ought to sound when you're hauling a full load up a steep grade is the kind of driver I learned to be.

That's the sweet life for me and it's the only thing I've ever wanted to do since. When I came back home after those six years in the army, I thought sure I was going to get me a good steady job driving for a trucking company on the highways from one end of the country to the other. Like I said, that's what I wanted to do more than anything else in the world and I still do and always will. But I ran smack-head-on into trouble. They won't hire me. They don't want nothing to do with my color.

I used to get a job now and then driving a puny little half-ton pick-up for somebody and doing some hauling around town, when there was some trash hauling to be done, but the way it turned out was that a white man always came along who wanted a job and they'd take it away from me and give it to him. After that the only steady work I could get was washing and greasing cars at the filling station Fridays and Saturdays—if you can call that steady—but I don't want to spend my life working part-time at anything. The way it is now, I can't make enough money to rent a better house for my wife and three daughters and there's never enough money to buy the clothes they need. I hate to see those three girls go off to school every morning dressed in put-together clothes like they have to do.

All I live for is to see the time come when I can get me a real job pushing a three-axle tractor-trailer down the highway and rolling it to Florida and back to New Jersey and then off to all the other places the white drivers can go. They haven't built a rig yet that's too big and heavy for me to handle—and the bigger the better. I know the driving laws from start to finish. I can follow the by-passes and truck routes through any city. And I've never ditched a truck I was driving or crowded a passenger car off the road in my life. I aint boasting about it—I'm just saying how it is. But I can't get that kind of job. They say I aint the kind of driver they need. What they mean is they don't want a Negro to work for them. Then they tell me I don't know how lucky I am to have a steady part-time job at the filling station on Fridays and

Saturdays. They know they aint fooling me with that kind of talk, but they say it, anyhow.

I ask them how come what I learned in the army about truck driving don't count. And they say the same thing every time. I'll tell you about that. You know about the highway truck stops and cafés everywhere you go. They're plenty of them all over the country. Anyhow, all of them in this part of the country used to have the nigger-go-away sign on the wall. WE RESERVE THE RIGHT TO REFUSE SERVICE TO ANYBODY. Some places have taken them down, but that don't mean a thing even when the civil rights laws say they can't make you leave. They'll find a way to keep you from eating. They can give you a little shove and then claim you're scuffling. That's all. Then all they have to do is phone the sheriff or the highway patrol and say you're disturbing the peace or something like that. You know what that means to a black man like me. A big fine, or the jailhouse, and maybe both.

The white-man superintendent at the trucking company mentions that every time I speak to him about getting a driving job. He says the company can't run the risk of letting a truck load of valuable freight left stranded on the highway for anybody to steal while I go to jail for scuffling in an eating place. He says he can't help it none, because it's not his business to go all over the country and see to it that Negro drivers can get in truck-stop bunkhouses and eating places and not go to jail.

That white man knows I'm a good driver. He said so himself. Once I got him to let me take one of the company's big tractor-trailers out on the highway for three or four miles, and then when we came back to the loading dock, he said I was a heap better driver than he was himself and sure wished he could hire me. That's exactly what he said. But he didn't hire me. He said he was sorry about it, but just couldn't do it as long as things stayed the way they are. I asked him how long did he figure that was going to last. He said only God knows for sure and God won't talk for fear of making some white folks so mad they'd stop going to church and paying the preacher.

He was real friendly about talking to me and that's how come I mentioned to him that nearly every town on the highways has eating places for Negro people and I could stop at one of those kind to eat and not go nowhere near the places where white people don't want me. He said he knew all about that, but it still wouldn't do. He said the heavy trucks his company runs have to stay on their routes on the pavement and not be pulled off on dirt streets where they might get mired down in rainy weather or tip over in a ditch while I was eating.

I reckon he was right about that. Nearly everywhere you go the eating places for the colored are on a side street nowhere near the main highway. I learned about that when I was driving in the army and I know what could happen to ten tons of truck on a soft dirt street. I wouldn't want to take a risk like that and see my rig get ditched and harm my driving record. It just wouldn't be like me. Anyhow, there ought to be some way to go about it so a colored man can work at that kind of job. It just don't seem right to me like it is. Any man on the highway ought to be able to stop and eat and wash up once in a while without risking a scuffle and ending up in jail for disturbing the peace.

The civil rights laws can say certain things, but some white people can figure out ways to get around the law. I don't know what's going to happen from now on, but something's bound to, because our people are working at it as hard as they can. When the young people started sit-ins and things like that all over the country, it didn't look like it'd amount to much at the time, but that's turned out to be a big boost ever since. The way they go about it might not look like much, but every inch counts, because the colored people never had even a toe-hold to start with.

And now we've got a real good toe-hold. Some of the old people are scared to their bones about it for fear of making the white folks mad, but that's all right. I can't blame the old people for being scared, because they've been bossed by the white folks all their lives and don't see how times can change. The young colored people are getting a good education these days and nothing's going to scare them. That's the best thing about it these days for all us colored.

The big trouble right now is because the white

folks have got the habit of having their way about things and they still take first-call. I don't say all whites are like that. A lot of them are on our side. It's the ones who do the most talking and get it printed in the newspapers who make the worst trouble for us. One of the things they boast about all the time is building some fine schools for our children, which is true, but that's still not enough. They stop right there and don't do a thing about getting the teachers better educated in the colleges. Most teachers don't know a bit more than the children have already learned. I know about that, because my three daughters go to high school and I hear all about it.

It's those same politicians you read about in the newspapers who won't let me drive a truck from here to Florida for a load of oranges and stop to eat when I'm hungry. I don't want to eat in their fancy cafés and sleep in their fine motels. That's what they keep on saying we're after. Looks like they'd know that a man like me, even if I had a good-pay trucking job, wouldn't waste my money doing that just for the spite of it. I've got too much sense to waste hard-earned money like that.

I'll tell you what I'd do with that money. I'd take it and rent me a house I'd be proud for my family to live in. And it wouldn't be over there in the white folks' part of town, neither. I'm just proud enough in my own right to segregate myself over here on this side with my own people.

3

It would not be unusual for an unsuspecting stranger in Bisco Country to find himself feeling sympathetic toward the conviction of a native-born white Southerner who argues, with all evidence of sincerity in voice and word, that he is the best friend the Negro American will ever have in this world. He is evidently convinced, and he would have a stranger believe likewise, that the Negro himself knows by experience, and willingly accepts the fact, that his only opportunity for happiness and security is possible when he lives in segregated social, political, and economic isolation.

Either with or without a twinge of sympathy for such a conviction, a first-time visitor soon becomes aware that this point of view of the racist-minded white Southerner is traditional in the Deep South.

It is a state of mind that has dominated Southern life for many generations. From the beginning, the feudal attitude was motivated by assumed racial superiority and indisputable economic selfishness; and later, shamed by the appalling evidence of feudal treatment, the Southern attitude was slightly adjusted to provide for fashionable expressions of pity and compassion for the Negro. Nevertheless, in the years following the Civil War, and regardless of motives, well-meaning or otherwise, the Negro still had no choice other than to exist in a modified form of slavery.

For the next hundred years in the agricultural South, and in particular wherever cotton was grown, slavery by intimidation continued to be the way of life for the Negro. By necessity working for token wages, he was unable to earn more than a mere minimum of food, clothing, and housing. Thus after freedom from a century of physical bondage, he was immediately enslaved in economic bondage for another century.

During all this time, Negroes were looked upon as being hostages of fortune or predestined orphans of inferior parentage who should be forever grateful for being protected from a hostile outside world. Payment for protection by their self-appointed benefactors was required to be rendered in groveling obeisance and uncomplaining servitude. Withholding food and clothing or the use of the lash could be the punishment for failure to make payment. And when this was not enough to bring about compliance, nightriders or the Ku Klux Klan could be called upon to enforce rule by fear.

A new generation of Negroes, educated and aware of their human rights, came of age in the Racial Sixties and rebelled against continuation of imposed isolation and discrimination. This awakening of a once docile race is disturbing to traditional attitudes of Southern whites from South Carolina to Louisiana. Century-old traditions are threatened with extinction.

As a consequence, one white Southerner will become a self-styled nigger-hater and white supremist; another, more politically astute, will cater to a calculated moderation of racial prejudice; and others, who claim a majority, will loudly proclaim that they know what is best for the child-like Negroes and vow to guard them against dangerous agitation by outsiders who have no understanding of a situation indigenous to the South. Though presently outnumbered, there are men of perception and foresight throughout the Deep South who are striving to make it possible for the Negro American to obtain his rightful first-class citizenship.

There is a wide belt of fertile mulatto soil lying diagonally across the central region of South Carolina between the northern sand hills and the southern coastal plain. This rich land was first put under cultivation in the eighteenth century by Gullah slaves working from the Pee Dee to the Savannah rivers and creating fortunes for scores of plantation owners.

This mulatto soil, so named for being a mixture of sand, clay, and organic loam, is ideal for growing tobacco, cotton, and grain. Even the great wealth extracted from the earth in the decades of slave-labor plantations failed to exhaust its richness, and now in these centennial years of the Civil War, scientific and mechanized farming is making the yield from the land even more valuable than it ever was in the past.

This modern agricultural operation progressively replaces hand labor with chemicals and machinery, and the descendants of Gullah slaves are gradually forced from their jobs and homes. As earning of the worker decreases, his standard of living goes down and down; he becomes another victim of modern poverty in a land of plenty.

Displaced by chemicals and machinery and his cabin bulldozed into extinction by other machines to provide additional acreage for farming or pasturage, the Negro field laborer has no choice to make. Inevitably, he and his family go to the nearest town as a place to live and to seek employment. There, as is probable, he will live in a dilapidated house of two or three rooms on the segregated southside. If he is fortunate, he will find seasonal farm work for a few months during the year, or he may be able to find occasional work tending lawns or collecting trash. And while he and his family are existing in squalor, all around him will be the fertile mulatto land producing its new abundance of wealth.

The native-born white Southerner, a devout Protestant in his mid-fifties and eighth-grade educated, sits on the counter in his small grocery store and talks earnestly about his convictions.

I know what I'm talking about and it's time everybody else knows the truth, he said. We take good care of our colored people. If you hear them complaining about something, it's because outsiders put them up to saying it—or thinking it.

That's why we don't want those part-white Geechees from Georgia coming over here. I don't know none of them by name and wouldn't want to. One of them might've been named Bisco or all of them might've been called that. Anyway, some of them say they're preachers and others claim to have a college education, but all of them are trouble-makers just like the white Yankees with their mister-nigger television shows. You know what I mean. It's those television shows that come down from the North with mister-niggers shaking hands and cutting up with white people—Mister Sammy Davis, Mister Harry Belafonte, Mister Louis Armstrong, Mister Nat King Cole. That's the kind of thing that puts wrong notions in our colored people's heads.

I'll tell you how good we treat the colored. Just last year we set aside some of our best city land and made it into a park just for them so they'd have a separate park just like the white people do. And that's not all, neither. We've built new schools for them with our own tax money that are more modern now than the old ones the white children have to go to.

Now, you can see why colored people don't have the right to complain about how they're treated. If anybody has a right to complain, it's the white children who have to go past those fine modern colored schools on the way to their old run-down ones. The colored people would've been satisfied with the schools they used to have if it hadn't been for all the agitation by the government in Washington about providing the colored with new school buildings as good as ours after we worked for what we've got all our lives and they didn't. It wasn't a fair thing for the people in Washington to make us take our tax money and do that. It looks like the votes these days somehow end up going to the wrong kind of politicians.

An elderly Negro laborer wearing tattered overalls and shredded shoes came into the store and bought a pound of lard and a bag of grits. As the storekeeper took the money and put it into the cash drawer, he told the Negro to be sure to hurry back as soon as he had enough money to buy something else. Waiting until the Negro had left the store, he said that colored money was just as good as a white man's money and that he was always glad to get as much of it as he could.

I don't know why it is that there's so much talk against us down here in the South, he said. It's bound to be either ignorance or meanness, though. You read in the newspapers all the time these days about somebody up North saying we discriminate against colored people. You saw me take that colored money just now. I sell to the colored just like I do to anybody else. I couldn't stay in business to the end of the month if I didn't sell to them. I'd be a damn fool if I didn't. Half my trade is with the colored.

I don't know what in hell's wrong with them up North. Trouble-making people up there are always saying we make the colored live where we want them to live and won't let them live where they want to. That's not the way it is. Colored people are used to living among themselves and that's the way the good ones want it to be. We don't have a single law keeping them from moving to a house in our part of town. There's no law saying they have to stay down on the southside, neither. When you have a good custom like we do, the government has no business making laws, neither.

It just wouldn't happen that some colored people had enough money to pay high rent or buy a house in our part of town. The colored people are just too poor to do that. They have a hard time paying a few dollars a month rent to live in their part of town as it is. I own a few houses down on the southside and I know how hard it is every month getting them to pay me what they owe. They're always complaining that they want city water piped inside the house and a flushtoilet instead of an outside privy or that the roof leaks when it rains or that the front porch is about to fall through, but that's only their way of trying to put off paying the rent when it's due and I don't pay no attention to that kind of complaining.

There's no need to worry about a colored doctor or school teacher or somebody like that getting rich enough to rent or buy a house in the white part of town. That's nothing at all to worry about and I can tell you why. All the property in our part of town belongs to white people and you won't see white people renting or selling to the colored. Nobody of us would do a thing like that. I know that for sure.

Here's how I happen to know it. Some of us got together one night not long ago with the real estate people in town and talked it over. All the real estate people said on their word of honor they'd never touch a deal like that, no matter how much money it cost them in commissions.

When we had this meeting, somebody asked what would happen if an estate came up for settlement and under the terms of the will the law required that a certain piece of property in our part of town had to be auctioned off to the highest bidder. That's a serious thing, because if there is such a provision in a will, it's enforceable by law. But that didn't bother us for long. Some of the lawyers at the meeting told us how to get around it.

What they said was for us to take care of anything like that in a quiet, orderly, business-like way and there wouldn't be no trouble at all. I'll tell you how the lawyers said for us to go about it.

If one of the colored out-bid everybody else and got legal ownership of a house in our part of town, some of us would have a serious talk with him and

convince him he'd better listen to what we said and
sell it back to us in a hurry.

That might take time and a lot of serious talking,
because he might have the backing of some trouble-
makers somewhere, but we'd pressure him enough till
he ended up selling to us. We'd remind him how good
we've been to his people in the past and tell him we'll
keep on being good to them as long as they cooperate
with us. We wouldn't let him forget about the colored
park we set aside just for them and the big new high
school we built for them with our own tax money.
And we'd tell him we'd hate to have to take all that
back.

Then we'd remind him how we arranged for the
colored to have a night of their own once a week at
the drive-in movie out on the highway east of town
so they could sit in their cars and see the pictures like
anybody else. Even if everything else failed to convince him, he'd listen to reason then for sure. The
drive-in movie is the one thing the colored don't want
taken away from them. That's the one big night of
the week for them now.

The good colored people know what we've done
for them and they don't want to go back to having
nothing again like they used to. Of course, there's
some trouble-makers among them who keep on saying
they want more and more all the time. That's the kind
who don't want to be satisfied with what they've got.
As soon as they get one thing, like a park or new

school building of their own, they turn around and say they want something more.

But, all in all, the good colored people will listen to reason when we talk to them. They're just like little children and you have to know how to treat them like you do your own children and give them some candy when you want them to do what you say. That's why, if we didn't know how to handle them, the colored in this country would go hog-wild in no time at all.

If the government in Washington would quit passing laws favoring the colored, we wouldn't have no trouble at all with them. Ever since I can remember, that café next door to here has had the no-service-to-colored sign on the wall. When the government says that sign has to come down to favor the colored, and the colored are let in, you won't find me in there mixing with them.

I do business with the colored here in my store, but they stand up and don't sit down and they leave as soon as they hand over the money for what they buy. And I'm not going to that café next door and sit down and eat with them. That's where I draw the color line and I'll be damned if anybody's going to make me step over it. They haven't got enough soldiers in the army to make me go against my principles.

And my principles are just as hard-shelled about living next door to them as they are about eating in the same room with them. Somebody mentioned at that meeting I was telling you about that everybody ought to be thinking about what to do if they sent soldiers here to help the colored to move in a house in the white part of town in case they somehow managed to get legal ownership of it and wouldn't stand still to listen to reason.

I don't know all what might happen, even if he did have the law of his side and the soldiers backing him up, but something'd be bound to. I wouldn't want to see that time come. Because I believe in peaceful living with the colored as long as they live separate. But if he went ahead and moved in anyhow after he'd been warned, and then wouldn't budge—well, there's just too many people in town like me who wouldn't stand for it once the sun had set on him.

I'm not coming right out and saying this or that about it now. But you remember that place in the Bible where it says something about somebody sitting on a pile of ashes. Well, that's what I'm thinking about right now. I reckon you know what I mean.

4

In the eyes of a twelve-year-old boy living many years ago in the Newberry County uplands of South Carolina, not far below the Piedmont Plateau, an uncle who said he knew the reason why all Negroes did not have the same shade of coloring was undoubtedly one of the wisest men in the world.

As I remembered Bisco several years before in Middle Georgia, he had mulatto-tan coloring of skin and I thought Negroes everywhere were more or less the same in appearance. Then one day at the railroad station my uncle and I saw a Gullah-speaking Negro who had come to Newberry County on the train from Charleston to preach at the African Baptist Church.

The evangelist with the shiny coal-black skin was no larger in size than any other Negro I had ever seen, and he wore ordinary clothing like everybody else, but he was so startlingly black that he looked as if he had been smeared with stove-pipe soot. I was sure he had come straight from Africa and not from anywhere in South Carolina.

My uncle had been to Charleston and he said he would recognize a Gullah-speaking Negro from the Carolina Low Country at first sight anywhere in the world. More than that, he said, he would be able to recognize a Gullah in pitch-black darkness without even being able to see him, because Gullahs spoke in a strange mumbling dialect of their own that even baffled other Negroes. He said if you wanted to hear what a foreign language sounded like, all you had to do was close your eyes and listen to Gullah.

The Negroes who went to the African Baptist Church were not able to understand a word of the Gullah preacher's sermon. They said he talked in such an unknown tongue that there was no chance of their being able to get religion in a whole week of preaching. Instead of staying to preach for a week at the revival meeting, he delivered only one sermon, took up only one collection, and then got on the next train to go back to Charleston.

As I recall what my uncle told me, the Low Country Negroes came to be called Gullah because that was the sound of the word they uttered when they tried to say they had been brought from Angola to America by slave traders. Since the Angola slaves on a Carolina plantation received no schooling whatsoever and had no opportunity to learn English, they created a dialect of their own by trying to apply the English pronunciation of their white overseers to the words of their African language.

My uncle said that after many years of associating with Gullahs following the Civil War the white people of the Low Country acquired the same Gullah dialect in order to be able to do business with them in stores and to give them instructions as servants and laborers. Ever since then white Charlestonians have always been able to understand each other when they talk, and Gullahs likewise understand them, but Carolina uplanders have never been able to comprehend much of what they are trying to say.

This was when I asked my uncle why some Negroes were brown or tan in color like Bisco and others were shiny coal-black like the Gullah preacher from Charleston. He said I was at the age when I ought to know about such things and that it was a good time to tell me.

First of all, he said he was not going to tell me what he thought was right or wrong about race-mixing, because the best education a man could get was in learning how to think for himself about such things so he could form his own conclusions about what was good or bad in life.

Then he said that when the first Negroes were brought from Angola in West Africa and sold at the slave markets in Charleston, all of them were as black as the Gullah preacher we had seen. Most of them were kept on the large plantations in the Low Country near Charleston and never got any farther inland than that, but that some of them were taken a hundred or two hundred miles away to work on the small farms in the uplands of South Carolina.

The slaves that were brought to Newberry County were spread over the country in small groups of one female and two or three males to a farm. The farms there were much smaller in acreage than the plantations in the Low Country and a farmer did not need as many slaves as the planter who owned thousands of acres. The reason why there were girls and women among the Gullahs when they were brought to the uplands from Charleston was because every owner wanted a female slave so that children would be born.

My uncle said this was a profitable system for the upland farmers. When the slave children grew up, they could be put to work in the fields or sold for a profit. By the time the Civil War ended, there were Gullahs spread over the whole state. And that was when the first mulattoes began to appear. The Confederate soldiers, and the Yankees, were the fathers of them, and whenever you saw a mulatto or quadroon or octoroon, you could be sure he would not have to reach very far back to claim kinship with a white family. He said he had seen quite a few whites and Negroes in Newberry County who looked almost like twins except in color.

I asked him what the difference was between a

mulatto and a quadroon or octoroon and why Bisco was much lighter in color than his mother and father.

He said I might not understand everything until I was a little older, but that the mixing of races was something I was going to hear about for the rest of my life and that I ought to know all I could for my own good how it came about.

The way he explained it was that if Bisco was lighter in color than his parents, it was because he had more white blood than they did. He said it was as simple as that. When you mix black and white, it's going to be some shade in between that will vary with the proportions of the mixture. When the races mix the first time, the color is likely to be brown, and then the color becomes a lighter tan each time the races mix after that. If the mixing is kept up long enough, somebody will eventually be light enough in color to pass for a white person.

Anyway, my uncle said, it's no miracle and there's nothing mysterious about it. It's merely a natural result. One way it happens is when a white boy living in the country or a small town like this one is too bashful or can't find a chance to do anything sexually with a white girl. But a boy can have a strong urge to do something about the call of manhood when he's fifteen or sixteen and a good-looking Negro girl might coax him just enough to let him know that she's willing for him to do what he wants with her.

When that happens, color won't have a thing in the world to do with it—it's girl you want. You know about some of the older boys going off to the woods in the daytime after school or hurrying to get out at night after supper. It's not always the same, because sometimes boys will make up masturbation clubs and put up a target to aim at. But a lot of times they go off like that because they're either looking for a Negro girl or already know where to find one. And then if she has a baby, there's another mulatto or quadroon born. Most white people don't like to talk about such things and pretend not to notice it, but it's something you ought to know about before you get to that age.

After that I asked him if white girls ever had mulatto babies. He shook his head emphatically.

I wouldn't say so. That time may come somewhere in the future, but right now in South Carolina it's something as rare as seeing an albino walking down the street. I've heard of it happening, but I've never seen proof of it. I don't know why it is, but white girls just don't seem to want to mix with the other race like white boys do. All I can think of is they must have a good reason for not wanting to mix. Maybe they're afraid they'll have a mulatto baby and be sent away from home to live somewhere in secret.

The risk of having a mulatto baby is one thing that would ordinarily stop a white girl, and they can be real strong about guarding their sex when they want to. Anyway, let's leave it at that, because I'm not going around asking them about it. That would take more nerve than I've got.

There was still one thing that had not been explained, and that was the reason why the Gullah preacher from Charleston was blacker than any Negro I had seen in any other place I had been in the South. My uncle, who had lived in Virginia and North Carolina, as well as in South Carolina, said he thought he could explain that.

Those plantations down in the Carolina Low Country were the largest of all and the owners were the richest, he said. The plantation owners contracted with the slave traders to buy Gullahs straight from Africa, kept them in herds when they worked the crops, and put them under lock and key at night. There were only a few girls and women among them —only enough to do cooking and housework—and when one of them had a baby, it was as black as the rest of them.

For another thing, the owners didn't need females to breed like it was done on the small farms in the upland country. The owners down there could buy new slaves at auction or have them shipped from Africa a lot cheaper than they could be raised on the plantation. It would've hurt their profits if they'd had to provide living space and feed young ones till they were twelve or fourteen years old and strong enough to do a man's work in the fields.

And there's still more to it. To keep the white overseers and guards from wanting to mix with the few Gullah slave females, which would've produced babies the plantation owner didn't want to be burdened with, they paid white women to come from England and let the overseers and guards pick and choose among them to marry. This is the main reason why the Gullah females in the Low Country never had a chance to have mulatto babies and why the race stayed pure black.

Then when the Civil War was over and the Gullahs were freed, most of them went straight to Charleston and never left it. Charleston was where they landed when they were brought from Africa, and maybe they thought they could get on a ship and go back there to stay.

Anyway, he said, Charleston is a pinched-in little place almost surrounded like an island by rivers and bays, and people who live there, white and Gullah, have grown to be satisfied to stay and die right there. A few Gullahs in Charleston who happened to be born mulatto are the only ones likely to leave it and go North. All this is why there're enough pure-blooded Gullahs in Charleston to keep them being the blackest Negroes you'll find anywhere this side of Africa.

I asked my uncle if he thought Bisco's parents or grandparents were Gullahs who had left Charleston and moved to Middle Georgia.

That wouldn't be likely, he told me. Gullahs never went far in that direction. They weren't the roaming kind. They stayed close to home even after being freed slaves. That's because they were always hoping that ship was coming to Charleston and take them back to Africa and they didn't want to miss it and be left behind.

The Georgia slaves were Geechees, and Geechees lost no time turning mulatto and quadroon and all the lighter colors. I don't know where they came from in Africa, but they were called Geechees to start with and they've been Geechees ever since. They were given that name because when they were brought from Africa and landed at Savannah, they were shipped right away up the Ogeechee River for a hundred miles and more and then auctioned by the traders to plantation owners all over East and Middle Georgia. Those plantations were a lot smaller than the ones in the Carolina Low Country and slaves cost much more delivered there than they did at the seaports. That's how they came to be so widely scattered over Georgia and so few of them to a plantation.

What made the real difference in Georgia, he said, was that female slaves were just as valuable deep in the country as males were because it was cheaper to breed and raise slaves there than it was to buy them in Savannah.

And one more thing. There weren't many white women in Georgia in those days, but there were plenty of Geechee girls. It stands to reason that the white owners would put them to doing housework and such things instead of sending them to work in the fields. What I'm trying to say is that the best looking of them were probably kept close to the house so they'd always be available day or night for sex cooperation.

And that's my theory why it didn't take the Geechees in Georgia very long to turn light in color.

I asked him if he thought a Negro like Bisco would be glad to be light tan in color instead of being as black as a Gullah.

My uncle said he had no way of knowing how Bisco felt about it, but that all the mulattoes and quadroons and octoroons he knew were uncomplaining about their color. He said some of them were so proud of their light color that they even had a high society of their own and that maybe Bisco would be a member of it.

5

The fertile farm land of East Georgia was a desolate expanse of human poverty in the nineteen-thirties. The countryside was devastated by merciless economic erosion. The people were ravaged by relentless hardship. It was a whole decade of wide-spread economic and psychological depression. Farm mortgages were foreclosed, business enterprises went bankrupt, doctors bartered services for chickens, lawyers gladly accepted fees in cows and hogs, life-long homes were lost to the tax collector, and hopes for the education of children were abandoned.

That era of hard-times in the nineteen-thirties is still vividly remembered by many people in Bisco Country as being the time of day-to-day struggle to get food for physical survival. Dollar bills that were passed from hand to hand became limp and thread-bare, and some of them were so tattered that they had to be held together with safety pins. The era will always be a shuddering memory to an older generation.

Now, in the nineteen-sixties, a full generation later, the rich mulatto land from the Savannah to the Flint rivers has the appearance of a country untouched in all its history by adversity and a younger generation has come of age knowing of the past only by hearsay. The rutted tobacco roads have been paved, cattle graze on the sloping green fields, diversified agriculture has replaced one-crop farming, modern brick homes have been built where once there were weather-gray wooden shacks, and industrial plants, large and small, provide jobs that never before existed.

A man who was born to the country sixty years ago and who has lived there through it all might be expected to appreciate the economic changes that have taken place during his lifetime and be content with his good fortune in an age of prosperity. He has thoughts, however, that disturb his peace of mind.

Standing now in the bright Georgia sunshine, he turns and looks thoughtfully at the shadow on the ground behind him. He is a retired farmer, sufficiently well-to-do by his standards, but he is not happy about the social and economic plight of those whose labor helped him acquire wealth and ease. His shadow is the symbol of his concern. He says he can never walk away from it.

I'll tell you what it is that bothers me, he says. Tourists coming and going through this part of the country between Florida and the North see only the front sides of things. They never know about the people behind it. They look at the cattle in the pastures and pass the fine brick houses along the highway and see the new factories in town, but they never have a chance to find out that there are people hidden from sight behind the hills and woods who have no share in any of it. Not a piddling dime's worth have those people back there got of it to call their own.

The people I'm talking about are the colored. They're the ones the tourists fail to see, and they're not hiding out on purpose. They are out of sight because they've been told to live in their segregated part of town or down the side roads in the country in shacks and sheds hardly fit to keep cows and chickens in.

That's right. The Negroes are even worse off now in these days than a lot of white people were in the worst days of the depression thirty years ago. The fear is that they'd get some of the money in circulation and keep a white man from getting it. That's why they can't open a store and try to get trade from white people. They can't get a job meeting white people face-to-face—unless you call collecting garbage that kind of job. They can't buy a lot and build a house, or rent one, neither, outside the place they've been told to live for the past hundred years.

If you mention my name around here, you'll hear me called a lot of names. You'll hear me called a crackpot, a trouble-maker, a lunatic, a nigger-lover, and a few other things, including being an out-and-out communist. They say I'm encouraging the Negro people to break down segregation and that if I know what's good for me I'll shut my mouth and keep it shut—or else move to the North or some other place like that.

But I'm used to hearing what they say about me and it don't bother me a bit now. I've lost some friends by speaking out the way I do and I'm likely to lose a lot more. My wife never opened her mouth about it one way or the other when she was around other people—she died not long ago—but they treated her the same way because of me right up to the day she died.

I don't worry about myself, now that my wife is dead and my children grown up and moved away. I've heard that some nightriders have been saying they're going to burn a cross in my front yard and nail a warning on my door, but that's not going to change my way of thinking. I've lived long enough and thought about it long enough to convince myself that I'm right. And when you've got the feeling that you're right about something, you don't have to boast about being brave—you just go ahead and do the way you think you ought to.

I grew up in this country with colored people and I worked side-by-side with them all through the big depression and right up to the time I retired a few years ago. You just can't know the Negroes like I've done for a lifetime and not treat them like you would anybody else. Not after you think about how you used to open up your dinner-pails together out there in a mean piece of newground or a blistering cotton patch and eat side-by-side with them in the shade of a persimmon tree at noon-time and listen to them tell you their troubles one minute and then tell a real funny story about something the next. And not after all the times when I've been too sick to get out of bed to feed my stock and have some of them come around to help out without being asked and then not take a dime for the favor they did. If you can't get along in the world with people like that, you've got a mighty sorry excuse for living yourself.

Once in a while, to be sure, one of them will get drunk and beat his wife and raise hell, but that's no more than what some white men will do. And every time you show me a Negro who went off and stole something I can show you a white man who stole just as much or more some other way. When it comes to things like that, I've yet to see any difference at all between the races except color.

It's claimed all the time that the Negroes are trying to figure out ways to take what the white people have got. But that's not exactly true. What they're after is to make the same kind of living the white people do. That's more like it. They want to get the things that are advertised for sale—like automobiles and furniture and new clothes. And they can't do that if they're not allowed to run a business in a part

of town where they can make money or if they can't
buy a farm with the kind of land that'll grow more
on it than chiggers and cockleburs and beggar-lice.

The storekeepers and farmers are scared of the
competition and fear the Negroes will get ahead of
them and make some of the money they're getting
now. The storekeepers want to take in the Negro's
dollar and the farmer wants him to keep on working
for next-to-nothing shares or wages. That's what the
trouble's usually about. And it's the same in town or
country. It's the scramble for money. Everybody has
to scramble for it, but everybody ought to have equal
chance.

You'll hear some people argue that the Negroes are
better off now than they've ever been before and
that they ought to be satisfied and quit complaining.

They'll argue that the colored people get paid in
money now, and not in flour and lard and old clothes
like they used to be. They'll say there hasn't been a
lynching in the county in thirty years. They'll tell
you about how their taxes went up to pay the cost of
new school buildings built just for the colored and
how much tax money it takes to provide teachers for
colored children.

All that's true enough as far as it goes, but times
have changed and it still don't amount to enough
when you look around and see how the colored have
to live in shacks and sheds all over the country.

Another argument you'll hear all the time is that
if you let the Negroes have an inch about one thing

it'll encourage them to do as they please about everything and take a mile. They say that'll lead to Negroes moving next door to white people and raping
your wife and daughters. If that's what they're after,
they would've been doing it for the past thirty years,
because they've been living out there in the county
on the farms side-by-side all that time.

The only raping that I know about being done in
this part of the country is when white men go after
Negro girls, and there's been plenty of that ever since
I can remember. Of course, it's not exactly fair to
call it raping, because any female likes to have a man
go through the motions of chasing her some. What
happens then is something that ought to be called
by some other name. Some want to be caught and
some say they don't, and that's why I wouldn't want
to have to decide what the difference was between
courting and raping. Either way, though, it's all for
the same purpose. I ought to know about that. I was
a young man myself once.

You've read a lot in the newspapers about picket-
ing and demonstrations and sit-ins and such things
in the big cities in Georgia. There hasn't been anything like that here yet and there may never be. The
reason I say that is because it's something for the big
cities where enough Negroes live to make it worthwhile.

In small towns like this, people know the Negroes
by name and they'd likely lose what jobs they did
have if they organized something like that. That's

why I think the best places for Negroes to work at getting the rights they're entitled to under the law are the big cities like Atlanta and Macon and Savannah where they've got plenty of students and others at the right age not to be scared off. Their young people are the best ones for it. Their old people are going to be cautious till they can see daylight.

Anyhow, no matter what the law says, it's going to take time. Make no mistake about it. There're plenty of white people in the cities who call themselves nigger-haters just like some do in the small towns, and they're the kind who'll find a way to make a lot of trouble for Negroes no matter what the civil rights law says. People who shoot doves out of season and bootleg liquor and steal gasoline from the state highway department won't pay much attention to the civil rights law.

The closest thing to that kind of trouble to happen here was when two Negroes from the North stopped in town and tried to get a room in a motel where the owner said he had no vacancies. I don't know if he was telling the truth or not about not having a vacancy in the motel, but, anyhow, the two Negroes started complaining and he called the police. The police took them to the city limits and warned them that if they came back to town they'd be charged with disturbing the peace and end up staying in jail for three months. They must have gone away because I never heard of a court case about it.

People who call me a nigger-lover and all the

other things say if I'd smell with my nose as much as I talk with my mouth that I'd change my mind in a hurry about the way I take up for the colored. You hear things like that all the time. What they claim is that the Negroes belong to a race that the law shouldn't allow to come anywhere near white people because they give off a bad odor. They don't call it odor, though. They call it stink. Nigger-stink.

Those same people claim there's something in the Negro skin that will hardly wash off, but if it does, the smell will come right back again the next minute as strong as ever.

Now, I'm no expert about a lot of things, and that's one of them. And I don't know what a real expert would say about that, neither. But if the expert was to explain it and proved it was true, I'll bet you it'd be mighty close to the reason I've figured out in my own mind.

I'll tell you what my theory is. It's something I'm convinced about for sure after working a lifetime side-by-side with both whites and blacks.

The darker a man's skin is—white man or Negro— the more he's going to sweat when he's out in the hot sun doing hard work. That's where nobody's sweat smells good and all sweat stinks. I've seen light-haired people with the palest kind of skin who could hardly sweat a drop when the rest of us had it running down our necks and getting our shirts sopping wet—and stinking so bad you'd puke if you hadn't been used to it.

On the hottest days of summer out there in the fields it was always the light-haired and pale-skinned in dry shirts who complained the most about the heat. They'd say they had to go sit in the shade ever so often to keep from getting a sunstroke while the rest of us kept on working in the heat of the sun and sweating with no trouble at all.

That's how I learned that anybody who sweats easy can work harder and longer in the sun than any other kind. I don't know how it is in other places in the world and if the same thing holds true, because I've never been away from here to see for myself, but I know what happens here in Georgia.

I've got real dark skin for a white man—and some people will say I'm eighth or sixteenth Geechee and could pass for white if I wanted to. Anyhow, I know how much I sweat. I sweat just like any Negro does. And you can't tell me that one man's sweat smells better than the next man just because he happens to belong to one race instead of another. If you believed that, you'd be the kind who'd believe a sweating Baptist smells different than a Methodist. Or a Democrat smells different than a Republican.

I'm not going to say it happens to women the same way—depending on whether they're light haired or dark haired. I remember hearing it said that women don't sweat, anyhow—they only perspire. So all I'll say is that heavy sweating is going to make a bigger stink for anybody than just a little bit of sweating—or perspiring.

6

On the geological terrain map, Atlanta is located on sinuous oak-wooded hills at the stony edge of the Piedmont Plateau in North Georgia. On social, political, and educational maps, the sprawling city is situated in a region where the contrast between the progressive and the reactionary attitudes of all the Deep South is clear and sharply defined. In the category of population, it is the metropolis of Bisco Country.

It has long been the tendency of Atlanta's climate to inspire the family of man to propagate and nourish—without compunction—the extremes of progressive integration and reactionary discrimination. In such an environment there can be very little middle ground for the uncommitted man to stand on, and, as a result of this distinct division, Atlanta has come to be the prototype of contemporary urban Negro-white civilization in the United States. Cities everywhere could profit by a study of the causes and effects of Atlanta's racial conflicts and social harmony.

Since there is undoubtedly a clear-cut dividing line between Atlanta's two extremes of conflict and harmony, there must be a good and sufficient reason for it. The reason is an obvious one. On one side is white-race economic and social frustration erupting in irrational violence in words and acts. On the other side is white-race tolerance and intellectual perception. The tug-of-war between the two forces has been long and arduous.

The plight of the uneducated and prejudiced white Southerner, or poor buckra, as he was sarcastically named by the Negro long ago, is a pitiful one. This man of ill will is between forty and sixty years of age, barely literate due to lack of educational advantages in his youth, who is economically handicapped in life because he is now and has always been an unskilled laborer.

One of the common evidences of the poor buckra's frustration is his gullible eagerness and fanatical desire to be duped by inflammatory exhortations of the designing, scheming, rabble-rousing, opportunistic, professional politician. These are the shrewd politicians who pander to the poor buckra's prejudice for the purpose of perpetuating themselves in office.

Having little within himself in which he can take pride, and habitually frustrated by his awareness of his past, present, and future economic and social poverty, the poor buckra resents any achievement of the Negro and retaliates by doing anything within his cunning to restrict and deny the rights of all Negroes. It is not unusual for men of such prejudice to instigate wily and overt violence in an effort to enforce and perpetuate racial injustice and discrimination.

The urbanized Atlanta Negro, in contrast to the frustrated poor buckra, is the fortunate beneficiary of the most extensive educational complex of any American city. This educational system has been segregated from the beginning, not by the desire of Negroes but by the discriminatory customs of the politically dominant white race.

Atlanta's many schools, colleges, and universities for Negroes came into existence as the result of determined efforts of Negroes themselves to provide higher education and professional training for Negro teachers, lawyers, and doctors barred from enrollment in the public and private institutions reserved exclusively for the white race in the State of Georgia. This determination to provide higher education for Negroes has made possible the present trained leadership of authentic spokesmen for civil rights in Atlanta, in Georgia, in the South, and throughout the nation.

A forty-five-year-old professor of history in one of Atlanta's Negro colleges has the calm confidence of an educated man who strives to attain an ideal by gentle persuasion and temperate argument. He is a tan-skinned octoroon, being of East Georgia Geechee and South Georgia white ancestory, and without bitterness toward fanatical advocates of white supremacy and racial discrimination.

It took us a long time, he said, and we're on our feet at last. But now that we're on our way, there's one thing we don't want to forget. The progress of the Negro up to this point is due to the collaboration by the enlightened younger generation of whites and the Negro religious leaders. That's why we were able to come to life after waiting a hundred years since slavery for what turned out to be nothing. And now we've got something for the first time in the Negro American's history.

I'm convinced that without the leadership of our ministers in the beginning we would've been the blind leading the blind. That means we would've made mistakes in judgment and walked right into damaging excesses. We've had little, if any, political leadership in all our history. But, fortunately for us, we did have the Negro preacher to guide us with his kind of experienced leadership when we began taking our first steps toward racial freedom.

The Negro preacher I'm talking about was not always an educated man, but, one of the educated or not, he was a thoughtful man. He advised our people to seek equal rights slowly and within reason and he himself went along with us to sit-ins and demonstrations—and to jail, too—but all that time he was cautioning us to keep our heads and not be tempted to resort to force and violence as a policy. This was the kind of leadership we needed at the critical stage when we were emerging from bondage and had the opportunity to consolidate our social and economic gains.

If we can keep this ideal of persuasion in mind and not resort to violence, it won't be long before we get our complete democratic freedom as Americans.

But there's danger ahead. There's already evidence that well-meaning but hot-headed fanatics—and I mean Negroes themselves—are trying to get rid of the calm and proven leadership of the Negro preacher, charging him with being slow-footed and behind the times, and institute a gangster-type racket by putting goons and hoodlums in his place. The white man can jeopardize his cause, too, just as much as the Negro, by indulging in violence.

Maybe I have this attitude about it because I'm not a black man. Some white people have the idea that all Negroes have a common ancestry. That might have been said about African slaves two hundred years ago, but not about us today. I'm a Geechee man myself—a Georgia-born octoroon—and I'm proud of it. This is why the Negro blood in me wants to keep the peace with the white blood that shows in my skin—or vice versa, if you wish. Judging from what I've heard about Bisco, he and I have a lot in common as Geechee men. Wherever he is, I'm sure he's striving to keep peace within himself just as I am.

Anyway, I'm convinced that we can gain more for ourselves by persuasion—since we are a minority—and gain it sooner—than we can by violence. This is something that can only be done by voting in every election. Our religious leaders know this and they are constantly reminding us of it. This is why more harm can be done to our cause by hot-headed Negroes throwing their weight around than by the rabid white supremists. You can't make anybody be your friend by pulling a knife or pointing a gun at him.

As it's been, we've had set-backs when we tried to integrate a school or a hotel or a restaurant, but that was only temporary. History teaches that time is on our side. That's been proved. It was only a very short time ago when the law of the land forced Negroes to ride in Jim Crow railroad coaches and at the back of the bus. It was Jim Crow this and Jim Crow that wherever a Negro went. All of that's now been wiped from the books and a Negro can even sleep in a berth on a train if he's got the money to pay for it.

And another thing. Only a short while ago it would've been impossible for a Negro to get a room in any Atlanta hotel or motel and sit down to eat in the restaurant. But now, if he's suitably dressed, he'll be accommodated nearly everywhere he wants to go.

The main trouble for us in Atlanta is that there are still some die-hard and over-my-dead-body hold-outs who maintain segregation and so far have been able to resist sit-ins and demonstrations. It's going to take the civil rights law to budge them, and they'll go to court and try to get delays on that, too.

Some of those white people run advertisements in the newspapers boasting about their segregation policies—intimating that the Civil War of a hundred years ago may be revived if we don't go away—and defying fate to force them to conform to the realities of the twentieth century.

We're using persuasion on those die-hards, and time and civil rights laws are on our side. We've come a long way already in just a few years and we're proud of what we've got so far. But that doesn't mean we're going to stop now and be satisfied halfway. The only thing we'll settle for now is total accomplishment.

Sometimes I get to thinking how ironic it is that in our segregated part of Atlanta, over here on this side of the railroad tracks, we have Negro-owned restaurants and night clubs with Negro performers attracting so much white patronage that on busy week-end nights Negroes sometimes have to be turned away at the doors because white people have taken up the seating space.

So when you talk about integration, don't forget that white people of Atlanta came over here and integrated our restaurants and night clubs a long time ago without even going through the formality of asking us if we had any objection to being integrated by them. Of course, we think we do have the best night clubs and singers and musicians in Atlanta and we're proud of it all.

The white people can't be blamed for wanting the best in night life, and they're always welcome and they receive special attention. Just the same, it is an ironical situation to have our clubs integrated by some of the white people who make violent protests when we say we'd like to enter some of their places of business over on their side of the railroad tracks.

White merchants want our trade, and they advertise for it in Negro newspapers, because anybody's dollar is worth exactly one hundred cents. And yet they claim they ought to have the right to draw the color line at the lunch counter and the washroom door in a department store.

The real hardship of Negro life is in the country and small town and not in the city. I know about this because I've lived in all three places. I was born in a South Georgia small town and lived on an East Georgia sharecrop farm until I came to Atlanta to get an education. It's the same in Alabama and Mississippi. In the larger cities, such as Birmingham and Mobile and Jackson, Negroes have been having their troubles with integration and civil rights, just as we do in Atlanta, but for the most part the Negro's social and economic bind is in the country and small town. That's where a colored man can be too scared to call his soul his own.

Very little is heard about life in the country. The big city gets the newspaper headlines when something happens in the Negro slums. Just the same when you break down the Negro population figures in the Deep South, the country outnumbers the city two to one. Servants in small towns, restaurant kitchen-boys, sawmill hands, day-wage laborers, and sharecrop farmers are so dependent upon their jobs for housing and survival that they live year after year in subjection to the whims of their white employers. Negro urban life is concentrated in side-by-side dwellings and floor-upon-floor flats. That makes it much more conspicuous than that of twice as many people living in desperation elsewhere.

I don't mean to say our people are physically mistreated in the country and small town any more than a poor buckra is mistreated. Whipping and lynching are becoming things of the past, thank God. What does happen, though, is that as Negroes they are the victims of a kind of psychological hardship or bondage. I'm talking now mostly about the older generation—those who are forty and fifty and older. The white employer tells them to take the pay offered, the housing provided, the working conditions demanded—or he'll get another boy who will.

And there are always other boys waiting in line for a job, too.

That's the kind of system it is. It's maintaining a pool of subservient people to work at the lowest possible rate of pay. This keeps the average country and small-town Negro in economic distress and makes him constantly fearful of risking his livelihood by speaking up for his rights. And this is why there's so little public protest or demonstration outside the larger cities.

However, a change is on the way. The younger generation of Negroes in the small community—those in their teens and attending school—are growing up without this fear. They'll be the ones to do what their parents and grandparents were unable to do.

Education is something new and exciting to young Negroes everywhere. The doors to the world are opening before their eyes, revealing sights their parents never knew existed, and they have the spirit and enthusiasm of pioneers to explore it.

In my time, when I left my father's sharecrop farm in East Georgia with four half-dollars in my pocket and somehow managed to get to Atlanta, there was no schooling down there for us higher than the fifth grade. That was as far as anybody down there could go in those days.

It's a lot different now, of course. We have our high schools and colleges all over the state and the young Negro is getting his education. However, Atlanta is still the center of higher education and our colleges and universities here are the goals of the ambitious ones.

But this is not a dead-end for students. Southern-born Negroes still migrate North and West in search of a better social environment and more economic opportunities. What we try to do is give them the best possible education so they will have a better chance to succeed in getting what they want wherever they go.

That's why I like teaching. It's a satisfying feeling to know that I'm helping this generation to learn how to be good citizens in the North and South.

7

The long, scrawny, emaciated, poverty-shriveled arm of Appalachia thrusts southwesterly from West Virginia through Kentucky and Tennessee into Northern Alabama. After this hopeful long reach over the border of Bisco Country, the supplicating hand of poverty opens palm upward for some token of sympathy. But it is too late for alms. The last coins of the kind-hearted have already been dropped into an imploring hand somewhere else with all sympathy spent.

The bone-hard thumb of the hand of poverty is the Arkadelphia Mountain in the Appalachian Range and its calloused soil covers all of Walker County in Northern Alabama. Like the four bony fingers of the Raccoon, Blount, Oak, and Beaver mountains which reach hopefully toward Birmingham and its outcroppings of coal and ore and limestone, the Arkadelphia region was never in its history an agricultural country.

The thin-soil gravel hills in Walker County are barren lands and the rocky ledges stubbornly resist the roots of vegetation. Whatever humus does accumulate under scrub pines and blackjack oaks is soon washed away by mountain rains and carried down the Warrior River to the Gulf of Mexico.

In the beginning, long before the Civil War, the Anglo-Saxon settlers came to the gravel hills of Walker County in search of cheap land. They found with ease what they sought and then, unfortunately, they were misled by the false promise of its brief summertime luxuriance. After that, with all money spent, they had no choice other than to make it the homeplace of their families. Now, after many generations of inbreeding, it is the birthplace of the handicapped people of Alabama's Appalachia who are rarely able to find anything but misery at home or away.

The time has not yet come when such barren land on gravel hills can be industrialized to furnish employment for its people. There have been many attempts made without success to establish industries.

Cotton mills have been built and abandoned; furniture factories were built and abandoned. The prospect of failure was obscured in the beginning by the optimism of success, but it took only a short time to realize that it was uneconomical to install industries in a remote region that had neither access to supply nor local sources of material for manufacture. The one remaining hope of the people is that sometime in the future science will find a profitable way to convert scrubby pine and yellow broomsedge into paper and plastic.

After the failure of cloth and furniture manufacturing, other attempts, both realistic and visionary, were made to find a way for people to exist on such unproductive land. But home-tufted bedspreads and hand-braided scatter rugs soon glutted the tourist market. There was so much over-production of moonshine whisky that a man soon lost hope of being able to swap a gallon of corn liquor with his neighbor for a pig or to take a jug of it to the crossroads store to barter for a can of snuff.

Then, even more recently, came the time when a vagabond shirt-and-skirt sweatshop would open overnight with several dozen sewing machines in an abandoned barn and pay wives and daughters thirty cents an hour to stitch and hem mill-end cotton cloth. That short-lived industry came to an end when federal minimum wage laws eliminated that occasional source of cash income in the gravel hills.

The economic plight of Jasper and Cordova and other small towns in Walker County is not unique in this extreme southwestern region of Appalachia. Similar distress exists wherever the gravel hills of Northern Alabama have been eroded by mountain rains until only a few inches of topsoil remain to sus-

tain scrubby pines, blackjack oaks, yellow broomsedge, and May-pop vines. But as if to compensate
for its hostile soil, the region is not lacking in an
abundance of old-time religion of the whoop-and-
holler sects and the die-hard politics of the run-nigger-run white supremists.

The affable, congenial, reddish-bearded storekeeper at the fork of the road in the intervale was
eager to talk about life and hard-times in the gravel
hills of Walker County.

I went to school off and on past seventeen, he said,
and that was long enough to read and write past the
sixth grade. But the best part was after I quit school
I married the school teacher who could add, sub-
tract, and multiply figures without never looking in
the arithmetic book to go by.

There was talk about it all along between here and
Jasper—about a white man like me marrying her—
and it still comes up now and then, because she sure
don't look pure-white like most white people do. She
told me she looks like she does because she's part-
Indian from Middle Georgia. I took her word for it
from the start, even if some people do still claim
she's dark-skinned like a part-white Georgia Geechee
and trying to pass for all-white. But that don't bother
me none. Not a bit. Marrying that school teacher was
the smartest move I ever made in my whole life and
I'm satisfied.

I asked her once what county in Georgia she came
from, but she said she didn't know because her folks

brought her to Alabama when she was too little to remember. I never heard her say if her daddy was Bisco or anything like that, but it might've been for all I know. She won't talk about kinfolks no more and it won't do no good for a stranger to ask her about it.

Anyway, what she did was give me her year's pay when she quit teaching to marry me and set up house-keeping. I took that money and went to Jasper and bought a whole load of canned goods and staple groceries and a few other things like nails and hinges. Then I hauled everything out here to this little old store I built out of sawmill slabs all by myself. Not many folks lived out here at the fork and hardly none of them had money to spend for canned goods and staples. But nearly everybody had a way of somehow finding a little cash to spend for snuff and so I hauled some of the canned goods back to Jasper and swapped for all the snuff I could get.

Getting that snuff to sell set me up in business right away and I never let the stock get short since. My wife was smart enough to learn me how to make the right change for a quarter or half-dollar so I wouldn't cheat myself every time I sold a can of snuff. That started about twenty years ago and now I can make change as good as any storekeeper in Jasper or Cordova. Of course, now, I don't have no big turn-over like the other storekeepers, but that means I don't have as many chances to make mistakes, neither, and short-change myself if I happen to count wrong.

The other big thing my school-teacher wife helped me out about was how to get along being poor like everybody else in the same fix. Everybody needs a true saying to fall back on when things get too discouraging and I didn't have nothing like that till my wife provided it for me. When I'd complain about something or another and said I wished I could get hold of enough extra money to fix up the store a little bit, she'd say to me to quit worrying about it and be satisfied like it was. She had a way of saying something that calmed me down every time. I'll tell you about that.

My wife sounded so educated when she said what she did that it made me want to learn it from her exactly. And now I can say it almost as good as she can. She says it just like I'm going to say it now. You listen to it. Poverty is a relative thing because it's kin to so many people in the world.

For a while I couldn't figure out just what it meant when it was said like that. Anyhow, I went ahead and learned to say it from her and now it makes me feel satisfied as soon as I say it to myself.

One of the times when that saying helped a lot was when there was a big train wreck. A few years ago a freight train jumped the track on a curve on the railroad about two miles from here near Cordova and three of the box cars loaded with sacks of flour and all kind of canned goods rolled off the track and busted wide open on a rock ledge down at the bottom of a high bank. I tell you, that's a sight you don't see a lot of in a lifetime. Anyhow, it wasn't long before everybody for miles around heard about it and hurried down to the wreck with every kind of sack, poke, and tote-bag you can name.

Those people loaded up with all the sacks of flour and canned goods they could carry off. And then they didn't stop at that, neither. They made as many as four or five trips, some of them. And they done that all night long, too. There was a creek down there where the three box cars busted open just like a May-pop when you step on it in June or July and all those canned goods got good and soaked in the creek water before they could all be carried off.

Anyhow, what I'm getting at is that all the paper wrapping came off of the cans soaking in the creek water and the folks who carried them off home couldn't tell what in the world was on the inside of them. But that didn't make no difference, because it was all free even if folks never knew when they opened up a can to eat if it was going to be beans or hash or some sort of juice. That made eating-time a pretty little trick to try and guess what you'd be putting in your belly.

But that's only part of what I started out to tell you about. It all leads up to the main thing, though. What that was was that the folks around here got so much free flour and canned goods they didn't have to buy none of that from me here in the store for almost a whole year and all I could sell them was a little snuff now and then and maybe a box of matches and a quart of coal oil and a few nails and some strap-hinges. Things got so bad for me with hardly no money coming in that I couldn't help but complain to my wife about it. There's nothing like hard-times to provoke a man to talking.

Now, I told you before that my wife was an edu-cated school teacher when I married her, and she never lost none of her education being married to me. And so when I complained to her about people not buying much to speak of, she said that same thing again you know about. Poverty is a relative thing because it's kin to so many people in the world.

I'll tell you, when a man gets to know a saying like that by heart, it's a mighty comforting thing, because the next thing you know you've got your mind off what you started to complain about. Of course, you keep on being poor as the devil like you always was, but having the comfort of an educated wife makes you able to go along with it a lot better than any-thing else could. I don't know if a rich man needs an educated wife, but it sure makes things tolerable for a poor man like me.

Maybe rich men don't have much of a chance to find out about it, but I know for a fact that an edu-cated wife is the best kind to have around the cook-stove and in the bed besides when there's an argu-ment with the preacher.

And I'll tell you why. I got to arguing with the preacher over at the church not a long while ago and he made me so mad I could've jumped him right there and then if it wasn't for my wife. The way it

ended up just goes to show how much good an educated wife can do for a man. I had my coat off and
was getting ready to haul off and beat hell out of
that preacher for saying I wasn't acting religious
enough to suit him, but she told me to put my coat
back on and go home with her and let her calm me
down likes she knows how.

That all got started when the preacher said everybody in the church got down on the knees except me
when he was praying and that a man who failed to
do that needed religion more than anybody else.
Even before I left home and went to church that
Sunday I told myself I was wearing the first new suit
of clothes I'd had for seven years and I wasn't going
to get down on no floor and get the pants all baggy
in the knees the first time I wore them.

Anyhow, I told that preacher I'd whoop and holler and put a little something extra in the collection
box but I wasn't going to ruin a brand-new suit getting the pants baggy in the knees so soon. He got all
shaky and shouting and said a man who talked the
way I did ought to go to hell and stay there when he
died.

It was right there and then when I shucked off my
coat and would've jumped him if it hadn't been for
my educated wife. She said she wanted to take me
home and calm me down. The preacher said he
wanted her to stay after me and everybody else left
so he could talk to her in private about my religion.
She told him she wouldn't do that, because it was
plain to see he was looking her up and down with

poontang in mind. If she hadn't been an educated school teacher, and if I hadn't been watching, he could've got her where he wanted her for sure.

Everything worked out just fine after that. The preacher left in a couple of weeks and went off somewhere else and the new preacher who came along said he wanted everybody to stand up in church while he was praying and not get down on their knees on the floor.

Keeping me from fighting the preacher wasn't the only thing my wife had a hand in. Like it is, the politicians come around every year or two wanting promised votes, and just last spring one of them walked in here and paid me a dime for a soda pop and then started talking big like God Almighty who'd bought and paid for both me and my wife's votes. He stomped around on his feet and said he was keeping the black folks in their place and not letting them get a chance to think they could act as good as white people. After a lot of that kind of talk he said me and my wife's votes would help him keep up his good work against the black folks. That made me mad as hell and I'll tell you why.

It was the way that politician came in here and spent a dime and then acting like he was doing me and my wife a favor to keep the black folks from acting like they was as good as white people but not asking me if I wanted that kind of favor done. He kept on talking like that about the colored and I got madder and madder.

That's when I opened up and told him if he was so set against the Negroes and all colored people he ought to move clear out of Alabama himself and go somewhere they wouldn't bother him. He said I talked like a nigger-lover and ought to be ashamed of my white face and that the whole state would go to hell and ruin if it wasn't for politicians like him who kept the black folks from going to the same schools and churches with whites. Then he ended up saying if I didn't vote right he was warning me that he'd get some men he knew in Jasper to come around some night and straighten me out for my own good.

I don't take that kind of talk from nobody, not even a big politician, and I told him to get the hell out of my store and stay out.

Right then was when my wife happened to come in the store and she could tell right away how mad I was about something. She knew what to think about it, just like the time I was fixing to jump that preacher, and she went straight behind the counter where I keep my old shotgun handy in case it's needed. She wasn't saying a single word when she picked up the gun and breeched it open.

The politician took a good look at her and asked me who she was. I told him who she was and he said she didn't look all-white to him and then wanted to know if I was race-mixing with a half-black. Just the same, even if he was a pure-white politician, I could see him looking her up and down with her kind of poontang in mind.

I was about to tell him plenty about minding his own business when he looked again and saw my wife holding up that breeched shotgun. She'd only done that to take out the two shells so I couldn't kill nobody, but that politician didn't know that. He thought she was loading the gun and he got out of there so fast he left his hat behind.

While he was getting in his car, my wife ran outside waving his hat at him, but he wasn't taking no chances. He got his car started and turned it around to get back to Jasper. I grabbed the shotgun and jammed the shells in the barrels and then fired both of them up in the air one after the other.

When the politician heard the gun go off, I reckon he thought for sure he was getting shot at, because he ducked his head down as far as he could and drove that car up the road making so much noise it sounded like a gravel truck stuck in a mud hole and trying to get out.

The whole thing about it was I'd forgotten about that shotgun when my wife came in the store, but she remembered it as soon as she saw how mad I was. All I had in mind was to brain that politician with the empty soda pop bottle for trying to buy me and her votes for only a dime and then saying my wife's looks didn't suit him for politics because she's not all-white. Maybe her color didn't please him for his kind of politics, but he sure had his eye on her for the other thing. He acted just like the preacher when it came to that.

8

Early in the nineteenth century, long before the Civil War, an act of Congress provided a land grant of several townships in area for two hundred French colonists to enable them to establish a settlement in America. Inspired by the revolutionary American theory of democratic government, and exiled from France because of their political beliefs, the colonists sailed across the Atlantic to Mobile and then came a hundred and fifty miles up the Tombigbee River in Western Alabama to seek realization of their dreams.

Being imbued with the spirit of democracy, and true to its principles of human freedom, the colonists brought no African slaves to the settlement they founded on the cliffs of the Tombigbee and which they called Demopolis.

It was in retaliation for their exile from France that

the refugees used the Greek language instead of French to create an appropriately descriptive name for the place they expected to live in democratic freedom.

Demopolis, or The People's City, was an idealistic experiment that failed so disastrously that all now left to show for it is the name of the town itself. The deceptive black topsoil, which became known as the Black Belt of Alabama, covered a rock-like hardpan of white clay only a few inches below the surface and was not suitable for growing grapes and olives as the colonists attempted to do. Besides, the malarial climate brought early death to men, women, and children, and there were no slaves for the hard labor of producing cotton in subtropical heat.

In the end, with their language being their only remaining possession, the few colonists who survived the ordeal returned to France after the Napoleonic Wars. Cotton planters, bringing their Guinea slaves from nearby plantations, were quick to take over the abandoned land.

Now, a century and a half later, Demopolis is just another Alabama town of less than ten thousand people with an equal number of white Protestants of Anglo-Saxon origin and third- and fourth-generation descendants of Guinea slaves. Ironically, all of them, both white and Negro, are dominated by the antithesis of democracy—the lingering traditions of plantation slavery and white supremacy.

Since the only remaining evidence of the French

colonists' idealistic effort is a place name—The People's City—it would not be unlikely if that too were obliterated. The possibility is that some of the white citizens, perturbed by the implication of the town's name when translated from Greek into English, will successfully petition to have it changed from Demopolis to Wallaceville.

There were several people seated at tables in the roadside restaurant and eating a native noonday dinner of fried pork chops, black-eyed peas, cole slaw, and chitterling cornbread. And of course drinking the traditional year-around Deep South beverage—iced tea and sugar. On the wall, draped with a battle-size Confederate flag, there was a large framed placard in colorful show-card lettering. A black mourning band had been fastened to the gilded frame.

WE RESERVE THE RIGHT TO SEAT OUR
PATRONS OR DENY SERVICE TO ANYONE.
ANY PERSON CREATING A DISTURBANCE
ON THESE PREMISES AFTER BEING DENIED
SERVICE WILL BE PROSECUTED.

The ingratiating, fiftyish, florid-faced real estate salesman had finished eating his noonday dinner and a quick smile of concern came over him as he glanced at the elaborately-framed and flag-draped memento on the wall. He was one of the civic leaders of Demopolis. He had acquired that distinction by being a member of several businessmen's clubs, chairman of a white citizens' committee, a bank director, a

Methodist, and by belonging to the country club and a fraternal lodge.

Such an impressive list of memberships and activities is just about average for a white citizen having the distinction of being known as a prominent civic booster in a Deep South town the size of Demopolis or a city as large as Birmingham. Doctors and lawyers rarely have the inclination to devote themselves to such a variety of activities, but merchants, bankers, and salesmen know that they have a better opportunity to make money if they become aggressive civic boosters.

It's a sad thing about that sign up there on the wall, he said. But law or no law, and even if what it says can't be enforced like it used to, it's worth preserving just like the Confederate flag. Maybe it won't keep blacks from coming in here, but it'll keep them reminded of who's still boss in this part of the South.

I'll tell you what the whole trouble is. It's all because people in the rest of the country just don't understand the racial situation down here. They're ignorant about it and we've got to educate them by showing them how to manage it. People up North think the blacks ought to be treated like anybody else and they criticize us for the way we handle them. They'll learn some day that we know more about it than they do.

What they don't understand up North is that niggers—or Negroes, as they say it—haven't gone through evolution as far as white people. They're still primitive—just like wild Indians used to be. They just don't have the intelligence we've got and it's going to take time for their brains to grow bigger so they can go through their cycle of evolution like we've already done.

We're letting them get educated now, but that's only a start. It'll be three or four generations from now before their brains are fully developed like a white man's. That's why it don't make sense to claim they ought to be paired with a white man when it comes to voting and living in the same part of town and everything else they say they want to do. It'll be another hundred years before they can complete their evolution and grow more brains and be ready for things like that.

It's just like I said. We know how to handle the blacks. We've been raised up with them and we know what's good for them better than they do themselves. I can take you over to their part of town and you'll soon see what I mean. The older ones— the real black Guineas—never went to school a day in their life. They can't even speak English enough for you to make out what they're trying to say. It's all Guinea-mumble.

That's the reason you won't find niggers from Georgia living in Demopolis. They can't understand Guinea-talk and they'd keep on the move till they got to Mississippi or somewhere else. You could spend a whole week in Demopolis looking for somebody named Bisco and still wouldn't find him or any half-white Geechee. I never heard of a nigger with a name like Bisco, anyhow. And if you asked me, I'd say a name like that is too good for a nigger in this part of the country. We make our niggers have real common names and keep the good ones for white people.

We call our niggers Guineas because they came straight down from the old-time Guinea slaves brought over here from Africa to work on the cotton plantations in Alabama and that's why all the old ones, and most of the young ones, too, talk a kind of Guinea-mumble. When we work with them, we can make them understand what we want them to do, but that's about the limit you can go with them as far as talk is concerned.

Now, it stands to reason they don't have the right to pair their votes with white people. They don't know any more what the voting's all about than a cross-eyed hoot owl. When the blacks get educated in a few more generations from now, then you'll be able to reason with them so they'll learn the right way to vote. But even that's a long way off.

Right now the blacks talk among themselves about civil rights and integration. I've overheard some of that and most of them don't even know what such things mean. I've heard some of them say civil rights was going to let them move anywhere in town to live next door to white people and integration was going to give them the right to pick out a white woman to marry.

If trouble-makers would only leave things alone, we could get the blacks educated in a few more generations and keep them in their place in the meantime. But it just don't make sense to say we ought to let them go to the same schools with white children here and now—no more than saying they can live next door to you and marry your daughter.

It's not that we don't want them sitting in the same school room and mixing on the playground with our children just because they're black and we're white. That's not the real reason. It's because they don't have the brain capacity to learn as fast as white children do and that holds the white children back so the colored can catch up. That's the only reason we don't want integrated schools now.

A big criticism you hear from outsiders is that we mistreat the colored people down here. That's just not so. There's not a bit of truth to it. If anything, it's a big lie. We've got some Southern customs you don't find in other parts of the country, just like people elsewhere have some customs that we don't have—and don't want, neither.

I'll grant you there was a time when a Guinea would get flogged if he was sent to the field to do certain work and then didn't do it like he ought to. And maybe one of them would get a beating if he didn't pay off some little debt he owed a white man or if he claimed he was too sick to show up for work. But as far as I know nothing like that's happened anywhere in Marengo County in the past eight or ten years. Outsiders who criticize us like that are unfair, because it gives us down here a bad name we don't deserve any longer.

Now you take this thing about us wanting to keep the colored out of motels and restaurants. There's a good sanitary reason for that. White people don't want to eat out of the same dishes they eat out of and we don't want to sleep in the same bed one of them slept in. That's the whole simple story. It's all right for them to cook for us and nurse white babies, but that's something we need them to do.

Everybody ought to recognize facts like that. When you've lived with your customs all your life, you don't want to give them up just because somebody a thousand miles away says he don't like them and tells you to get rid of them. That makes no more sense than for me to tell somebody up North I don't like boiled cabbage and baked beans for breakfast and say he's got to do like I do and eat grits and sow-belly every morning instead.

That proves there's a damn good reason for any custom and this thing of keeping niggers out of our restaurants started a long time ago and we learned them to know their place and they never dared step over the line. If the trouble-makers up North want to know the truth, we don't give a God damn what they think. This's the South, by God, and we'll find a way to run it the way we please.

But I'm willing to be reasonable and try to help them understand how it is. One thing they don't realize up North is that in this part of the South the blacks outnumber the whites in a lot of places. We're just about even here in Demopolis now, but they're gaining on us every day—even if we are bleaching them and their bastard babies get lighter in color all the time.

I'll tell you what would happen if we let them have the right to do as they pleased. Suppose you stopped at a motel here in Demopolis to get a room for the night and was told it was all sold out, but while you were being told that a nigger drove up in his car and got a room right away to sleep in because he'd already made a reservation in advance. Now, that's something that'd send a shiver running up your back and make your hair bristle and stand on end.

I'll tell you something about Northern people they sure don't even know themselves till they move down here to live. I've seen it happen time after time when a big company transfers a plant manager or sends a salesman to work the territory.

No matter where they come from up there, it takes no time at all for them to start thinking like we do about the blacks. In the beginning, before they get accustomed, they might say they don't see no harm in letting a black family move to a house in our part of town or letting the black children go to the white schools. But that won't last long. After they've lived here a while and seen some of the Guinea niggers around here they soon see the light and change their minds in a hurry. After that, when something along that line comes up, they'll back us up every time. That shows it's a natural thing for all white people to want to keep the blacks separate. Even the few Jews go along with that.

If you didn't know me better, you might think to hear me talk that I'm what some people call a nigger-hater. But I'm not. I get along with them fine as long as they stay in their place. I don't do much business with them, except collect some rents on a few houses I own over in their part of town. They don't have the money to buy the kind of real estate I sell, anyway.

There's not many people in Demopolis who have hard feelings against the black race. Those who do speak up about it in a sincere way are only trying to do what they think is best for the blacks and advise them to pay no attention to the trouble-makers and outsiders who're egging on the blacks to integrate the schools and churches and everything else that belongs to white people. People like us want to promote harmony between the races and we're working on it all the time.

If we can just put things off and hold our own in our lifetime, we'll be all right. The only trouble is that it looks like we're losing ground little by little. The government in Washington is doing everything it can to push us against the wall and make us give up by ranting and raving about civil rights and discrimination.

Every time the government in Washington makes a move like that, it encourages the blacks to put in a claim for more and more. Then the government steps in and helps them get what they want and it undoes all the good we do to keep things quiet and normal and the way they should be.

All I can say is that the people in other parts of the country had better wake up before it's too late and help the white citizens in Alabama, and all over the South, too. If we don't get some outside help, and a lot of it, we can't keep on carrying the whole load much longer.

What white people everywhere ought to do is vote the right men into office, just like it's done in Alabama and Mississippi, to run the government for us. If they don't hurry up and do that, and keep on doing it, the white people all over the country in every state are going to be sorry.

It'd be an awful thing to let the blacks chuckle and laugh about how they turned things around and put the white people in their place. And that's sure to happen if we don't watch out.

9

If there are places that can be called typical small towns in Bisco Country, there are several reasons why Jackson in Southern Alabama would be named as being one of them. There is even a good possibility that Jackson might be entitled to the distinction of being the most typical of all.

This pineland town has a population of approximately twenty-five hundred Negroes and twenty-five hundred whites; it is situated in the center of one of the Deep South's distinct geological zones; it is frequently a target for destructive winds in the broad tornado alley between the Atlantic Ocean and the Mississippi River; and its climatic extremes can bring sunstroke in summer and frostbite in winter.

The only reason that Jackson might be disqualified in a contest for pre-eminence among typical small

towns is because it is in Clarke County. Unlike similar local-option liquor-dry counties in Southern Alabama, Clarke County produces more moonshine corn
liquor than its people have the capacity to consume.

Fifty miles northward of Jackson are the rich
cattle grazing ranges and fertile lands of the Black
Soil Belt. Fifty miles southward is the varied agricultural plain of the Gulf Coast. Chambers of
commerce and civic boosters everywhere might un-
derstandably be envious of the town's stable and
prosperous year-around economy—pine lumbering,
brassiere manufacturing, and 'shiny whisky distilling.

But, typical or not, either economically or geographically, Jackson does maintain strict conformity
with the traditional racial customs of the Deep South.
The unwritten law of white supremacy is more
strictly enforced than the posted law on the parking
meters along the town's main street.

The white citizens of Jackson live on the bluff
above Bassett Creek; the Negro citizens live under
the hill in a country slum beside the sprawling saw-
mills. On the bluff are the wide, paved, tree-bordered
streets and modern houses surrounded by green
lawns; under the hill are the narrow, rutted, dirt paths
and sagging slab shacks clinging to the bright orange-
colored clay.

And, just as in many similar Deep South towns,
white citizens are quick to say they are ashamed for
visitors to see the squalor of the country slums under
the hill. Nevertheless, they are the ones who make

no effort to eliminate the enforced degradation of Negroes who continue, as necessity compels them, to pay ten or fifteen or twenty dollars a month rent to the white landlords on the bluff because they are prohibited by unwritten law to live elsewhere in a segregated town.

The elderly, gray-haired Negro storekeeper on one of the orange-colored clay paths under the hill has a meager stock of soft drinks, tobacco, and candy. His customers are Negro school children with pennies for candy and sawmill workers with dimes and quarters for cokes and tobacco. The light-skinned Georgia-born Geechee is almost seventy years old and he has lived in Jackson for nearly a quarter of a century. During that time he was a sawyer in one of the lumber mills on Bassett Creek until he was no longer useful when he became sixty-five.

I'm a Geechee and proud of it, he said. I don't claim that I'm better than the Alabama-born colored —the ones the whites call Guineas—but if anybody starts talking about their families and kinfolks, I'm going to put in a claim for my Geechee people in Georgia.

I grew up on my daddy's sharecropping farm in Coweta County in Georgia. That's where I was born and I lived there till I was about fifteen. I had three younger brothers and my daddy and mother said it was too late for me to get a college education but not for my three brothers. I'd been going to school till I was fifteen, and I got pretty far along with my education, but not enough of it to get me into college. That's when we left Georgia and moved to Alabama so my brothers would be closer to Tuskegee and have a chance to go to college later.

My daddy rented a farm about twenty miles from Montgomery and started raising cotton and I was big enough then to work right along beside him. My brothers went to school and raised pigs and calves at the same time so there'd be some cash money to save for their college education. That was enough to get started one by one up at Tuskegee and they worked at jobs in town and at the college so they could pay their way and graduate.

My mother was proud of them getting a college education but always sorry about me. However, all that time she was keeping after me to do all the reading I could so I'd educate myself as much as possible. That got me into the habit of studying and I never wanted to quit after that. That's why I always scrape up enough money right to this day to subscribe to two daily newspapers, one in Montgomery and one in Mobile. I found out long ago that the more you learn the more you want to keep on learning and I don't want to quit now. There's too much going on in the world for me to want to be left out of it.

Over there in Coweta County in Georgia, we lived on a little farm between Moreland and Luthersville, but I don't remember anybody named Bisco. A lot of colored people lived there then, and I might've known him, because I knew nearly everybody in muleback distance in those days. There was a light-skinned Geechee boy over there with a name something like Brisket or Bristol, and he might've been the one. We went to the same school together for a while, but I don't remember much about him now. That was a long time ago.

Before my mother died, she used to hear from folks in Coweta County, and she might've known who that boy was and what happened to him. A lot of colored people left Coweta County to live someplace better, and some of them moved to Alabama, too, just like we did. He might've been one of those who came to Alabama. The next time I run across people from Coweta County I'll try to find out if they know anything about somebody named Bisco or any name sounding close to that.

I traveled around a lot myself in my younger days after my folks moved over here to Alabama. I was in the army for about two years in the first big war. They sent me all the way to Europe for almost a year. Then before the war was over they sent me to a lot of different places all over the United States. That was a real good part of my education—finding out first-hand what it was like in the rest of the world outside the South.

After I got out of the army, I was a fireman on the Frisco Railroad for about seven years out of Birmingham and I stayed with the Frisco till they wanted me to move to Mississippi and work on a division over there. I always liked it here in Alabama, a lot more than working for the Frisco in Mississippi.

The white people over there in Mississippi treat the colored like dirt—and I mean dirt. A colored man can get killed for nothing in Mississippi—and a lot of them do. You see somebody you know one day and the next day you don't. He gets covered up in an old dry well or they weight him down with some scrap iron in a swamp. That's the best place in the world to stay away from—or get out of—if you're colored. I'm not saying it's good enough here, but so far it's better for the colored than Mississippi. That's why I left the Frisco after staying in Mississippi only a month and came back to Alabama and got a good job here at the sawmill.

After nearly twenty-five years right here in Jackson at the sawmill I liked it so much I hated to quit working when the company said I had to quit when I was sixty-five. That was about three years ago. I'd saved a little money all that time and bought my own house for my wife and me and our children. Which is a lot better than paying up to twenty dollars a month rent to live in the slab shacks the other colored people down here under the hill have to do.

All three of my children were girls and they wanted to get married instead of going off to college. I was sorry about that. A good college education is the greatest thing in the world when you're going to be colored all your life. But the girls wanted to get married and raise families of their own. I can't quarrel with them about that now. They're all settled and happy with their families. Maybe girls are meant to be smarter about things like that than a man is and know from the start what's good for them.

Besides saving enough money to buy my own house while I was working at the mill, I put aside enough to buy an acre of land and build my own store on it. It's all paid for now and I don't owe a dime to anybody. You can't have a better feeling than that when you get to be my age.

Of course, I don't make much money selling a little candy and tobacco, but it's enough for my wife and me. Best of all, I get a chance this way to talk to all the people in the neighborhood. Everybody comes in here to spend a nickel or dime once in a while.

Getting to know all the people in the neighborhood was how I got interested in doing something to help all the youngsters who live around here. They didn't have a real playground and there wasn't much they could do. Youngsters can get in trouble if you don't keep them busy—they start throwing rocks, if nothing else—and that's why I went to work and organized A Boy Scout troop for them.

Of course, I was a little too old to be the Scout-master. So I turned that over to a younger fellow I trusted. But I signed up sixty-two youngsters for the troop and cleared off some of my acre of land I didn't need and made tables and benches for them out of slabs they gave me at the mill. These young-sters here are too poor to buy the complete Boy Scout outfit and so what I did was see to it that every one of those sixty-two boys had something to show for being a Boy Scout. One of them would have a regulation hat, another one would have the official belt buckle, somebody would have the Boy Scout manual, and so on like that.

My three younger brothers who graduated at Tuskegee left Alabama a long time ago. Now and then one of them comes to visit me and tries to get me to move up North where they live. But this is my home right here now and it's where I want to stay. One of them is the principal of a school in Connecticut. One is a professor in Pennsylvania. The third and youngest of all is the pastor of a church in Michigan.

Except for being better educated, all my brothers are just like me in most ways. They stay with our race and don't try to live outside it.

I know a lot of colored people go to the North thinking they'll be living outside the race, but they soon find it just won't work out that way. As long as a man looks colored, that's the way he's going to be no matter where he lives and he ought to be proud of it. And if he's a Geechee like me, he can boast about it, too. The only real way the colored can live outside the race is to be light enough in color to pass for white, and that's something a real black man just can't do.

I know my color and I'm proud to stay with it and be what I am. Some of my grandchildren have got a lot lighter color than me and my wife and the time may come when they'll go up North to pass and leave our race. That'd be all right with me. You can't expect the younger generation to keep the same old-fashioned ideas I've got.

I was born and raised in the South and I've been colored for sixty-eight years. That means I've lived within my race all my life and I'm accustomed to it. And that's why you won't see me at my age getting out and demonstrating for integration and civil rights. That's something for the young people to do and I'm not going to blame them for trying to change things for the better as long as they use good common sense about the way they go at it. I'll stand behind them every step of the way as long as they do that.

What I hope about it is that our young people will stick with Martin King and listen to him. If it wasn't for Martin King, we'd still be back where we started from—which was 'way back nowhere. I don't want to see some scatter-brain colored people do the wrong kind of agitating and do us more harm than good. If everybody will listen to Martin King, we'll be all right.

There's something in the newspapers nearly every day about integrating the school so the colored and white children can get the same education. I'm in favor of both races getting a good education, but the big trouble is that nobody's going to get a good education if the schools don't provide better teaching.

It's a shame the way some of the white teachers misuse the English language.

Those teachers have been to college and they should've learned the correct way to use the language if they're going to be teachers. I'm not educated enough myself to explain what the right way to say something is, but I can tell when something they say sounds wrong. Maybe I ought to watch what I'm saying right now, but the way I feel about it is I wouldn't want my children or grandchildren go to a school and come out of it speaking the kind of grammar some of the teachers do. And I'll say that about any teacher—white or colored.

Some of the young colored people right here in Jackson are getting restless and say they want to do something about their civil rights and organize demonstrations and such things. So far, nothing like that's been done and some people like me keep on telling them not to be too quick about it. I don't care what the law says, this is still a white man's town. I'd want to hear what Martin King advised before starting anything like that in a little place like Jackson. Some white men never pay attention to any law and they can be real mean to all colored people when they want to be.

The way I see it, action like that ought to start in bigger cities like Birmingham and Mobile and Montgomery where the colored live in bigger numbers and have some good leadership. The young people in Jackson need a leader with real good judgment before they start something like that and right now there's nobody to take charge. Without some good leadership, the young people run the risk of not being able to control a demonstration up on the bluff where the white people are. That could start a race riot quicker than anything else I know of. And if things ran wild, all the colored would end up with more harm than good.

It's the same way about the Black Muslims in Jackson. Some of our people talk about wanting to join the Black Muslims, but there's no leader for them here so far, and you can't run that kind of organization without leadership no more than you can have a worthwhile church without a minister.

To tell the truth, I'm suspicious of the Black Muslims, anyhow. I just don't like their kind of talk. And when you look them straight in the face, they look mighty close to being something exactly like the Ku Klux Klan for the colored.

Some people argue that we need the Black Muslims to give Negroes the courage they need to stand up and claim their rights.

I'm in favor of us getting up all the courage we can, because that's what we're going to need a lot of from now on, but I'd feel a lot more comfortable with my courage if I got it from Martin Luther King.

Maybe it's because I'm proud of being a Georgia-born Geechee with my kind of tannish color, but anyway I always tell people I'm not black enough to be a Black Muslim.

10

To come upon it in the lingering twilight of a balmy summer day, Laurel is a languorous tree-shaded town with a name of romantic implications in the pine-crested hills of Southern Mississippi. Flowers bloom profusely in stately gardens and a stranger in town is likely to be mesmerized by the flower-scented air. Under the tall spire of an elegant church there is fervent praise of God, unoffending mention of the brotherhood of man, and a prayer for the less fortunate people in the world.

In the bright light of day, however, the reality of Laurel is made plain and revealing. It is then a place of thirty thousand people arbitrarily confined within inflexible zones allotted to wealthy white citizens on the northside, segregated Negroes on the southside, and impoverished whites in the middle.

Any such socially, racially, and economically regulated allotment of residence is not an unusual custom in Bisco Country. In fact, it is a traditional way of life rigidly maintained and enforced from South Carolina to Louisiana; nevertheless, the contrasts between classes and races are more sharply defined and rigidly fixed in Mississippi than elsewhere.

The stranger in town might say that Laurel, in particular, is remote and isolated from the mainstream of American life and that its people are pathetic in their solitude. But a prideful white citizen of the northside will insist that all of Mississippi, and particularly Laurel, has been endowed with a fortunate heritage that less privileged people living in other states scorn because of envy and ignorance.

All might be well in Laurel, as it could be elsewhere in Mississippi, if prideful residents of the northside would look at least as far away as the southside of their town even if they do not wish to see beyond the borders of their own state. As it is, and as though it is a way to avoid embarrassment, they fail to acknowledge their responsibility for the poverty and degradation of the Negro families on the southside and ignore the fact that it was the labor of Negroes that enabled them to accumulate wealth and social pretentions.

But customs prevail. And arrogance predominates. Instead of acting upon his responsibility as a citizen in modern America to alleviate and adjust economic and social discrimination imposed upon the Negro for generations, the white supremist is intent upon striving by any means to enforce a perpetuation of racial injustice that originated long ago in the time of slavery. As long as this custom can be maintained, the conscience of the white supremist will be quiet and undisturbed. Enforcement of the custom ranges from intimidation to physical punishment to violent death.

The Citizens' Council, or, as the white supremist organization is more aptly called, the White Citizens' Council, was founded as recently as the nineteen-fifties in Mississippi. The purpose of the organization is to legalize segregation and prohibit by law any form of integration and racial equality and to relieve the individual white supremist of the do-it-yourself chore of run-nigger-run intimidation.

The White Citizens' Council is a white-collar club striving by day in business suits—and often in judicial robes and clerical garb—to attain by subtle propaganda and forthright political pressure the same discriminatory results that the Ku Klux Klan might fail to achieve by night in bed-sheeted paraphernalia with acts of intimidation and premeditated violence.

In such a racist environment, membership in the White Citizens' Council quickly became a status symbol for both the dedicated white supremist and the political opportunist. And, because of the organization's unconcealed appeal to prejudice and opportunism, local chapters were soon founded in towns and cities throughout Mississippi.

Now, after ten years, there are White Citizens' Councils in all states of the Deep South and, in addition, there is a mail-order White Citizens' Council of America to sell memberships and provide pamphlets and insignia for the racist minded in all parts of the United States. In Mississippi and elsewhere, the only purpose of the organization is to incite racial prejudice and promote political action for the establishment of legalized segregation and discrimination in every state in the nation.

The dedicated advocate of white supremacy spoke with the fierce-eyed evangelistic fervor of a revivalist preacher at a country church in Mississippi on a hot summer night.

I'm going to tell you some plain facts. The fate of this whole nation is in the hands of people like us who are working day and night to keep the two races from mixing. That's us, by God, and you can look at me and say I'm one of them. And I'm damn proud of it, too.

We're working like hell to save the whole white race from getting wiped off the map. If we don't have segregation, and have it now, this'll be a nation of mongrels—not white like us and not black like them. We'd be a dirty gray color in between. It's up to us to put a stop to that for the good of the white race.

You hear a lot about integration and what a fine democratic thing it is and all that kind of damn radical talk. But we won't be fooled. We know it's the Yankees who're pushing it. It's a communist trick. When you first hear about integration and don't stop and think, you might even take it for granted that it's a natural thing to let the niggers live where they please and go where they please and do what they please. But when you come right down to it in actual practice, no pure-blooded white man is going to be in favor of it.

It's undemocratic to force integration on pure-blooded white people and make them mix with niggers. Segregation gives a white man the democratic right to choose the kind of people he wants to eat with and do business with and even talk to. That's why it's a communist trick to say whites and niggers ought to mix in all sorts of ways. I hope those Yankees get mixed and come out with the half-color they ought to be.

I've heard all the Yankee talk about people like us in the White Citizens' Council being nigger-haters and reactionaries and such things. But there's no truth to that. Not one little bit of truth. It's the same old communist trick to call us things like that. We're loyal white Americans who are brave enough to speak out and do something about the way the niggers are trying to move in on us and take what don't belong to them. We're a hell of a lot more patriotic than the Yankees who criticize us.

You hear the niggers say they want to sleep in our hotels and motels, but they don't have no more right to do that than go to my house and sleep in my bed.

They say they want to eat in our cafés and restaurants, but they don't have no more right to do that than they have to walk in my house and sit down at my table and tell my wife to feed them.

And it's the same about everything else they make a claim about wanting to do. You go ahead and give the niggers just one little foothold and there'd be no end to what they'd want next.

For one thing, every nigger man in town would want to bed a white woman. That's right. And it's not that they'd want to marry your sister, neither. What they'd want to do is strip her naked and then go on from there. Given a chance, they'd make whores out of all white women—and then tell white men to keep hands off. You let a crowd of niggers stand around on the street corner and watch a white woman walk by and you don't have to guess a second time what they've got in mind. You'd be right the first time when you said what they were thinking about was getting their hands on her titties and their balls between her legs.

It used to be that white men would go after good-looking young colored girls whenever they felt like it. There were plenty of them all around and easy to get between sundown and dark. They could always be counted on being better honeyfuckers than ordinary white girls, too. But that's not the way it is any more —there are plenty of easy-to-get honeyfucking white girls these days.

But what's happening now is that things have got

turned around and nigger men want white women. But nobody's going to tell me it's all right for a white girl to intercourse a nigger man. And anybody who'd say that is a Yankee and a communist and ought to be run out of the country.

All this proves we've got to keep up all the segregation we've already got—and even that's not enough in these times. What we've got to do is have more of it and make it stick. The way to do that is to find ways to make it legal by law so the government can't come along and put white people in jail for doing what we know is right.

The niggers don't know it, because that's how ignorant they are, but everybody else knows they were a hell of a lot better off in the old days when they couldn't even read and write. That's when they were trained to know their place and never made trouble thinking they were just as good as white people and ought to have the same privileges. That's why when you have hard-and-fast segregation it works for everybody's best interest—and for the niggers most of all. Then they don't have false notions when they're kept segregated—that's when they damn well know their place and stay in it.

Down here we get too damn much unasked-for advice from Yankees about how to handle the niggers. I don't mind being criticized by somebody who knows more than I do about something and who can show me where I'm wrong. I'm open-minded about such things. But what I don't like is being criticized by somebody who don't know what the hell he's talking about. Up there, Yankees won't likely see a nigger in a week's time and he lives as far away from niggers as he can get and won't eat in the same place with one of them even if the meal was free.

Just the same, the Yankee will be the one to make a big to-do about the way we say nigger children have got to stay out of our white schools and how we try to keep the race from eating in our restaurants and sleeping in white motels. But I'll tell you something about that. And I've seen it happen plenty of times. You let a Yankee come down here to live and he'll be the biggest talker of all in favor of segregation before the year's out. He don't want no nigger getting close enough to fool around with his wife.

The main thing we're criticized about all the time is what Yankees up North call civil rights. They're not really talking about segregation and such things when they say that. They've got segregation of their own up there and they want to keep it that way just as much as we do down here. What they're talking about is voting. They want to use the nigger votes down here so they can control our politics. That's the only thing they're after. They don't give a damn about whether the niggers go to white schools and sleep in white motels in the South. They're after the nigger votes and nothing else.

You hear those people up there swear-to-God and hope-they-may-die that they're sincere about all the other things they criticize us about. Like hell they are. It's just a trick to take over our politics and put their own politicians in the government in Washington from the president on down. And if they ever have their own way about it up there, white voters in the South might as well spend their time howling at the moon for all the good voting will do them.

I can tell you one thing that's sure as hell to happen and it won't be long, neither. The niggers keep moving to the North by the hundreds and multiplying twice as fast. And they're not doing it because they like living with Yankees up there better than living down here. They're moving up there where they can get jobs that pay them two or three times more than they're worth down here or anywhere else.

And so one of these days before too long the whites up North will wake up and open their eyes and see niggers everywhere—in their schools, churches, stores, houses, restaurants, and everywhere else they look. That's going to make Yankees stop and wonder what the hell happened. When they come to their senses, you'll see the Yankees running around like crazy and wringing their hands and trying to figure out what in hell they can do to keep the niggers away from them. They don't know it yet, but what they'll end up doing is the same thing we've been doing here right along—keeping the niggers in their place and making them stay out of ours.

You can tell that some of the smarter white people up North are already getting ready for that by joining the White Citizens' Council by mail and studying our way of doing things. There's no great number of them signed up so far, but they will. They're bound to as things get rougher for them every day. They know we've got the experience and know-how for dealing with niggers and they'll be coming to us and begging us for God's sake to help them out.

I wouldn't be surprised if the Yankees acted sheepish about it at first, after the way they've been criticizing us, but we'll help them out. A good professional always likes to help out amateurs when they're in a jam and show them how to do a thing right and proper.

11

The deep, dank, dark-brown alluvial soil of the flood plains of the Lower Mississippi River Valley covers a region of the Deep South fifty miles or more in width and nearly four hundred miles in length between Memphis and New Orleans.

The fertile alluvial deposits of humus, loam, mold, and mulatto-earth erosion, washed downstream to Bisco Country by centuries of rain and melting snow from the fields and forests of a third of the United States from Montana to Tennessee, created an agricultural paradise on both sides of the constantly flooding Mississippi River. But paradise would have been unproductive without Negro labor, and so first there was legally instituted slavery and then illegally imposed servitude.

This extensive region of alluvial flood plains,

warmed by sub-tropical climate and watered by abundant rainfall, has always been called the Delta even though the actual geological delta of the Mississippi is far to the south of it.

It was nature's unquestioned right to skim the richness of soil from a wide expanse of America and deposit it in the Delta. However, it was a questionable privilege that permitted plantation owners to acquire extraordinary wealth from the land by ruthlessly impoverishing the people who labored on it. Ownership of the land changed from generation to generation, but the feudal system went unchanged. The agricultural paradise also remains, as likewise does the family of man which has labored without equitable reward in a sociological and economic hell-hole since the days of slavery.

The Yazoo Basin is one of several flood plains formed by nature on the east side of the Mississippi River—and wholly within the State of Mississippi— and its plantation land is now securely protected from over-flowing river waters by dikes and levees. The Yazoo River itself—like the Big Black and the Bayou Pierre—is one of the many muddy tributaries of the Big River.

More than half of the people living in the Yazoo Basin are Negroes of Angola and Guinea slave descent who are employed seasonally for a few months of the year to plant, pick, and bale its cotton. However, even though the Yazoo Basin is thickly populated by Negroes, they are only a small portion of the Delta

Negroes living on both sides of the Mississippi River between Memphis and New Orleans whose extreme poverty makes ordinary American poverty elsewhere appear enviable by comparison.

The unemployed and destitute person of either race in a city slum or Appalachian ravine can stand in line and receive government-issued food stamps or welfare relief checks. Agricultural workers in the Delta, by unconscionable legislation, are excluded from government relief programs.

The unemployed and destitute Negro farm laborer in the Delta can only hope that the rumors he occasionally hears will come true and that he will be one of the fortunate who will receive a donation of food and clothing from somebody somewhere who is concerned about his plight and knows where to find him. Food and clothing collected in Memphis or Nashville by churches, labor unions, and civic clubs are always sufficient to spread a hopeful rumor in the Delta, but the supply has never been sufficient in quantity to reach all who hear of it.

There is want of food and clothing in many places other than in the Delta and able-bodied people usually manage by some means to survive hunger and cold. And in the Delta in particular, a meager amount of food of some kind can usually be found and clothing can be patched and held together. But lack of adequate food and clothing is only one of the misfortunes inflicted by poverty in the Delta Country. This is where definitions of poverty and destitution are to be rewritten for American usage.

A young Negro farm laborer and his wife and three children had lived on a cotton plantation four miles from the nearest Yazoo Basin town for several years. The dwelling, for which he was charged ten dollars a month rent, was a sagging, slab-sided, weatherwarped, two-room tenant house more than twenty years old. The glass panes of two of the four windows had been broken for many years and were covered with sheets of rusty tin that had been ripped from the roof by a windstorm.

The white owner of the land and dwelling had furnished no material for repairs and the tenant and his wife had chosen to protect the children and themselves from wind and rain by covering the broken windows with the tin roofing and to endure the leaking roof. The building was similar in size and condition to several other inhabited tenant houses spaced twenty feet apart in a row beside the muddy farm road. Behind each shack was a doorless lean-to backhouse privy screened with burlap sacking. There was one pump-well to supply water for all who lived in the settlement.

Unlike the cautious and suspicious older Negroes in the settlement who were fearful of the consequences of complaining about anything and risking the white landowner's wrath and vengeance, the young Negro talked freely and boldly about his life.

I haven't worked none for seven months since last

September and I'm five months behind in rent already. And me and my family are a heap more behind in eating than that. We're empty-belly people most of the time.

The white man promised me two months of cotton chopping and two months of picking this year and I'm going to stay around here for that. Then I'll leave for sure. My mind's made up good and plenty about that. I'll make me about five dollars a day for those four months and pay the white man the back rent I owe him for living in this shack and then keep up with the new rent till the picking's all finished.

Me and my wife don't want no more of this—working all summer to pay the white man a year's rent and going hungry-belly in this old house all winter long. That don't make sense. And it wouldn't do no good to move to town, neither. Rent's just as much in town and there's no more work there than there is here.

I'll tell you what I'm going to do. I'm going to New Jersey. I sure am. You can count on that. From then on I'll be through working for the white man for only four months a year and paying him rent twelve months to live in this shack and go hungry half the time, too. I'm going off to New Jersey and stay there. That's where I'm going to do my living—and not here no more.

I went up there to New Jersey once before. That was about two years ago. But I had to come back down here when my father took sick and I was sent

for just when he was dying. I had a fine job in New
Jersey working in a zipper-making factory and making two dollars an hour all the time I stayed there
and not just half that much working for the white
man down here for only four months the year.

My brother's up there in New Jersey and he got me
that job I had. He stays, too. He don't come back
down here none at all. He says he's a Northern man
now and don't want nothing to do with things down
here in Mississippi. I don't blame him none. He almost got killed to death once down here when a
white man got mad at him about a little nothing and
shot him twice with a shotgun. He was lying in ditch
water all night and the next day where the white
man thought he was dead and left him. But he
crawled out and drug himself a whole half-mile to
somebody's house to help him. That's why he won't
come down here to Mississippi no more.

When I finish up working for the white man four
months and paying off the rent, my brother's going to
send me the money so me and my family can move
to New Jersey and stay there like he does. That'll be
the big day. My brother lives in a fine place up there
that has a real bathroom and inside running water
and plenty of heat for cold weather. He wouldn't live
in a shack like this one here is. And I won't no more,
neither. Not after I finish up working for the white
man this time and paying off the back rent I owe.

The white man said to me he'll get the sheriff after
me if I move off the place and don't pay up all I

owe him before I go. But he don't need to worry none about that. I'll pay up before I go off. You won't see me getting trapped like that and put in jail and kept from going to New Jersey. I've got that too much on my mind.

I'd gone to New Jersey last year after finishing up working the crop for the white man and paying up the rent I owed then, but my mother's been ailing pretty bad and I've got to do something about looking after her first. She's got the insurance for the undertaker all paid up, but she don't have no insurance for a place in the graveyard. She lives with her sister in town and can't work no more to get money.

A heap of folks fail to think about that graveyard insurance before it's too late. I reckon that's because they've been on top of the ground all their life and fail to think about providing for where they'll have to be put in the ground when they're dead.

That's the only reason I'm still here now and not already up in New Jersey. But I'm going off just as soon as I can get that graveyard insurance fixed up for my mother. Won't nothing stop me this time to going up there to stay and work at the good job my brother's going to get me and make real money enough to eat and buy clothes for my family.

I don't have nothing much against the white man, except he won't fix up this old house and wouldn't let me dig a grave on his land to bury my father in when he died without the graveyard insurance.

I told the white man I'd do every bit the work myself fixing up the house and it wouldn't cost him nothing except for a little roofing and boards and a few nails. But he said he couldn't spend no money on no old house like this here that was going to fall down soon, anyhow. After he argued like that, I told him all he'd have to do was let me take some old roofing and boards off another old house of his that wasn't fit for nobody to live in. He wouldn't do that, neither.

I don't know if the white man's just naturally stingy or mean or don't care none what happens to the colored who work for him. But there's something like that bout it because he sure don't act right dealing with the colored. I said to him once the colored who work for him and pay him ten dollars a month rent ought to have a place to live in that don't leak through the roof when it rained and have busted windows where the field rats can get in and crawl all over you in the night.

But saying that to him didn't help none at all. It just made him mad. Spitting mad. He told me I'd better shut my mouth and stay quiet if I wanted to stay out of trouble. Looks like it don't never do a bit of good for the colored trying to talk to the white man about nothing. There's some fine white people in the country but he sure aint one of them.

My father lived down the road yonder in that fourth house and he'd worked for the white man and the white man's daddy most of his life right here on this plantation. He was better off than some of the colored who died on the place, because he'd paid the undertaker's insurance up. But he didn't have a dime's worth of the graveyard insurance.

That's why I asked the white man if he'd loan me twenty-five dollars to pay the graveyard for a place to bury my father in. The white man's daddy used to let the colored be buried somewhere on the place when they died, but the young white man wouldn't do that.

I promised the white man I'd work it out just as soon as the cotton was ready to chop and he'd be sure to get the money back that way. But he just wouldn't do it. There wasn't enough time left to write a letter to my brother in New Jersey for the money to pay the graveyard. My father'd already been dead two days then and the undertaker said it was the law that he had to be taken somewhere and buried in the ground before the third day was up.

My father had that fifty dollars' undertakers' insurance all paid up, but none of the graveyard insurance. That was the big trouble. The undertaker collected the fifty dollars of money to pay for the box and there wasn't none left for the graveyard. You don't know how poor poor can be till you get too poor to be buried in the ground.

When I couldn't get nowhere trying to make the undertaker let some of the money he'd collected pay the graveyard, that's when I came back out here from town and tried to get the white man to loan me the twenty-five dollars for the graveyard.

And that's when the white man said he wouldn't

do it. I told him how the undertaker said the burying had to be done right away that same day like the law said and that I had to get rid of my father in the box by sundown or he'd put them both out the back door in the alley and leave them there. The white man said it was my business to bury my father and none of his.

Maybe not many other folks know it, but that's how I found out there's no way of being poorer than when you're trying to bury somebody and can't find the money to pay for a place in the ground to put him in. You might think there'd be a free graveyard somewhere for people like my father, but there wasn't. They told me there's a graveyard in town where poor city people can be buried free, but none for the country people who die poor.

The neighbors along the road here wanted to help me out, but they couldn't raise that much cash money between them all. It was getting late in the day by that time and it wouldn't be long before sundown. That's when I went back to the white man one more time and asked him please if I could dig a grave and bury my father right here in the yard behind the house.

I reckon you might know what he said. The white man said if I dug a hole in the ground anywhere on his land and buried my father in it he'd bulldoze over it with a tractor so quick nobody'd never know where it was after that. I tried to tell him my father's grave wouldn't take up none of his farm land if he'd

let me dig it sort of under the porch or at the under-
side of the house, but he wouldn't hear to that,
neither. He said he didn't want no niggers buried on
his land and rotting in the ground.

Something had to be done about it quick after
that. Time was getting real short. The sun was only
about treetop high then and sinking fast. Three neighbors and me went down the road to the paved highway where the colored-man storekeeper had a little
truck and he let us borrow it and go to town and get
my father in the undertaker's box.

It was past sundown before we could get to town
and sure enough the box was out there in the alley
just like the undertaker said it'd be by that time. We
loaded it in the truck and got started back out this
way. The four of us got to talking about what to do
and the way it ended up was there wasn't but one
thing in the world about it to do.

By then it was a long time after dark with only a
little moonlight showing down and it looked like it
was getting ready to cloud up and rain some pretty
soon. We drove the truck off the paved highway
over to the side of it where it was widest and found
the highest place on the bank where it was dry above
the ditch and the standing water. That's where we
started digging with the shovels we'd brought along
and dug the grave deep and wide enough to put the
box down in it.

Nobody was a preacher or deacon in the church
and all we could do about it was stand there and

take off our hats and sing some of the songs. We didn't sing too loud—just enough to make the songs sound right—because some white people who lived in a house not far off might get curious and want to come down there and find out what was happening alongside the state highway in the nighttime. Then we shoveled in the dirt and covered the box good and tamped the sod back on top of it to keep it looking natural so the highway people or nobody else would be apt to notice it.

The only way to mark the place to remember where it was was with a rusty old Holsum bread company sign that fell off a post and we laid that on top of it. That bread company sign made it look just like a natural part of the state highway.

When you go from here back down to the paved road and turn toward town, you can find the place about half-a-mile that way. Look on the right hand side close to the wire fence where there's a scaly-bark tree and you'll see that Holsum bread company sign flat on the ground and right beside it a little bitty fruit jar with some flowers in it.

My wife goes down there every Sunday and puts some fresh flowers in the fruit jar because my mother can't get up out of bed to come out here to do it. What I'm doing now is paying a quarter-a-week graveyard insurance for my mother so when she dies she'll have a place in the graveyard to be buried in. She's already got the undertaker's insurance all paid for.

I just wouldn't feel right going off to New Jersey to stay and leave my mother here with no paid-for place in the graveyard. It wouldn't be right to put her down in a grave by the state highway after dark when nobody was looking.

They keep the sides of the state highway nice and grassy and the weeds chopped down, and they pick up all the beer cans people throw away, but I've made up my mind for her to have the kind of burying my father couldn't get. I want my mother put in the graveyard in the daytime with the preacher on hand and out-loud singing the way folks want it done when they have to die and be buried.

I don't know nothing about any colored man from Georgia or Alabama ever coming to this part of Mississippi. If he knows what I know, he'd stayed where he was or else kept on going to Arkansas. It might not be a bit better over there for the colored, but it sure can't be worse than right here.

If that fellow named Bisco asked me, I'd tell him to haul himself off to New Jersey like I'm going to do. I don't mind being born in the Big South, but I don't aim to be pushed to death in it.

12

For a long time the old Memphis road has been a
narrow trace, occasionally dusty but usually muddy
and rutted, that lies straight and flat on the soft dark
earth of the Delta and goes alongside the railway
tracks between Clarksdale and Coahoma in Northern
Mississippi.

It was a busy thoroughfare for carriages and wagons
long before the Civil War—and a profitable one for
highwaymen, too—but nowadays it is no more than
a back-country farm road between cotton fields. It
has been unmarked for travelers and little used by
automobiles since the construction of a paved highway several miles eastward.

Just the same, now in the nineteen-sixties, the old
Memphis road is still as muddy and slippery and
treacherous in rainy weather as I remember it being

forty-some years ago when it was the only thorough-fare for cotton-wagon teamsters and an occasional automobile being driven from Clarksdale to Memphis.

In the summer of 1918, during the last year of World War I, I was fifteen years old and for two months I had been driving the YMCA staff car at the military training camp at Millington, Tennessee, about eighteen miles north of Memphis.

Being the only staff-car driver and on twenty-four-hour call, I was often sent to the Millington rail-way station to meet a lecturer or musician traveling the YMCA's war-time circuit. More frequently, how-ever, I was awakened between midnight and dawn and sent to bring a stranded soldier back to camp from a Millington speakeasy bar or a madam's place so he would not be absent-without-leave at morning roll call. Once in a while a staff member wanted to go to church on Sunday and I took him to town and waited until the services ended.

However, my consistently regular duty that sum-mer was to drive the secretary or some other member of the YMCA staff to Memphis for the week end when he wanted to visit friends or spend his leave in one of the hotels.

After two months on the job my driving record was still good, having neither been charged with speeding nor involved in an accident, and the YMCA secretary said he was so confident of my driving ability that he wanted me to take the train to Clarks-dale and drive his own Ford touring car the whole distance of a hundred miles from his home back to Millington.

It was shortly after noon when I got off the train in Clarksdale on a Saturday in the heat of August. Within half an hour I had found the secretary's home at the address he had given me and I knocked on the door of the small white bungalow to tell his wife that I had come to drive the car to Millington.

The secretary's wife, who was slender and dark-haired and in her early twenties, opened the screen-door immediately as though she had been waiting for me to come. Then she said she had heard from her husband about my coming and had a dinner of fried chicken, field peas, sliced tomatoes, and spoon-bread waiting for me. She insisted that I would have to eat the meal she had cooked for me before I could start on the long trip back to Tennessee.

While I was sitting at the table, the girl ate nothing herself, and, while nervously fingering a knife and fork, she asked so many questions about her husband that it was an hour or longer before I could finish eating. She wanted to know why he would need their automobile in Millington when he had the use of the YMCA staff car; she wanted to know how often he was in the habit of spending the week end in Memphis; and she asked several times if he often left the YMCA in the evening and spent the night somewhere else instead of sleeping in the YMCA dormitory. I told her that I was always so busy with my duties of washing, polishing, greasing, and driving the staff car that I had no opportunity to know where her husband went or what he did when he was away from the YMCA hall and dormitory.

When I got up from the table, she said it was very late in the day and there might be an afternoon thunderstorm and that I could spend the night right there and leave early the next morning. She took me to a room where she said I could sleep and carefully smoothed the gleaming white counterpane on the wide bed. After a few moments she said that she and her husband had no children and that she was miserable being there alone all the time. When she looked up from the bed, there were tears in her eyes.

It was nearly four o'clock in the afternoon when I backed the Ford touring car from the chickenhouse shed at the rear of the bungalow and waved good-by to the girl as she followed me to the street. When I looked back at her the last time, she had put her hands over her face as if crying again.

I drove slowly through Clarksdale, stopping frequently to ask directions, until I had found the old Memphis road going northward alongside the Illinois Central Railroad tracks. The hottest part of the August day had passed, but the dark clouds of the thunderstorm the secretary's wife had warned me about were moving rapidly up the Mississippi River a few miles away as I began driving up the rough dirt road toward Coahoma.

During the first few miles I was able to go as fast as twenty miles an hour and I was confident that by driving all night I would be able to get to Memphis by sunup the next morning and then deliver the secretary's car to him at the YMCA hall in Millington soon after breakfast.

The afternoon thunderstorm was moving faster than I could drive on the rutted road and I began to wonder if I should have stayed in Clarksdale as the girl had begged me to do. I had gone about nine or ten miles when the rain suddenly began coming down in tropical torrents and it was too late then to turn around and go back. The ruts were soon filled with water and the windshield became so splattered with muddy water that I had to lean over the side of the car in order to see where I was going.

Then all at once the road was an endless mud puddle and the rear wheels began spinning help-lessly in the slush. Even then I thought I could man-age to keep the car going by driving slowly and carefully in the slick Delta mud. But suddenly I felt the wheels slide from the road and an instant later the car went into the ditch and turned upside down before I could get out and keep from being pinned under it. I heard the windshield crack and splinter at the same moment the oilcloth top was flattened upon me and the steeringwheel. At first there was a faint gurgling of running water not far away and then I felt it flowing against my head.

The engine had stopped when it was submerged in the ditch water and I could hear the beating of rain upon the overturned car and the frequent sharp cracks of lightening striking trees in the cyprus swamp beside the road. It was not long until I smelled gasoline leaking from the tank over my head and I was afraid the car would catch on fire.

When I tried to move, there was a stinging pain in my left arm. I kept on struggling to pull my arm free so I could crawl out, even though the pain became more intense each time I moved, and I realized that I was trapped under the weight of the car. Then, with drowsiness coming over me, all I could think of was the cool white counterpane on the soft bed in Clarksdale.

I remembered nothing after that until sometime during the morning of the next day.

When I opened my eyes and looked around me that morning, I was in a small narrow room with roughly raftered ceiling, unpainted board walls, a single window, and a large smoke-blackened brick fireplace. After that I could see that I was in a wood-posted wide bed and covered with a colorful patch-work quilt.

Gazing at the high-posted bed and patch-work quilt, and not knowing how I had come to be there, I wondered if I were dreaming or if I were actually in bed in Bisco's house in Georgia. Closing my eyes, I could see the room in Bisco's house as clearly as I had always remembered the night I wanted to get into his bed.

I had no idea about how much time had passed

when I opened my eyes again, but I saw a large and fleshy Negro woman standing at the side of the bed and watching me with solemn concern. Her skin was shiny-black and her heavy breasts lay on the bulge of her stomach. When she saw me look at her, she leaned over the bed and put her hand on my forehead. Her hand was cool and comforting and I hoped she would never take it away.

Presently she straightened up, her teeth gleaming with a motherly smile, and nodded confidently. Waking up and seeing her like that in a familiar-looking room, she looked exactly as I remembered Bisco's mother long before in Coweta County in Georgia when I wanted to spend the night in Bisco's house and sleep in the quilt-covered bed. I raised my head from the pillow and looked around the room to see if Bisco were there, too. Nobody else was in the room.

As I lay there wondering how I came to be where I was, I could remember the automobile sliding from the muddy road and turning upside down in the ditch. I knew I had tried to free my arm so I could crawl out, but I could remember nothing else after that. Staring at the rafters overhead, I began to worry about what the YMCA secretary would think about my driving ability when he found out that his automobile was upside down in a ditch beside the old Memphis road somewhere in Mississippi.

Presently a tall, muscular, mulatto-colored Negro wearing mud-stained overalls walked into the room and came to the side of the bed. He smiled at me, just as the Negro woman had done, as though glad that I had at last opened my eyes.

First, he asked me what my name was and where I lived, and then he told me that his name was Troy and that his wife was Mandy. While he was talking to me, his wife brought my clothes and laid them on the foot of the bed. Together with socks and underwear, my cotton khaki uniform had been laundered and ironed. My shoes had been cleaned, too, and my felt hat with the YMCA insignia cord around the hatband had been cleaned and dried and creased in its original shape.

The motherly Negro woman left the room and went outside where I could hear the voices of several children who were playing in the yard. Troy helped me to the side of the bed, saying he was sure that my left arm was only bruised and sprained and not broken, and that if it had been broken he would have gone to Clarksdale for a doctor.

While Troy was helping me get dressed, buttoning my shirt and tying my shoes for me, he told me how glad he was that I had not been seriously hurt when the car turned over and pinned me under it. He said it was lucky that he had happened to come along just when he did, or otherwise I might have been drowned in the rising ditch water.

By the time I had finished dressing, Troy had told me what had happened the night before. He said when the thunderstorm came up and drenched the ground, he had to stop plowing in a field about a quarter of a mile down the road and was almost home with his team of mules when he saw the car upside down in the ditch. He called several times, but there was no answer, and yet he was afraid some-body might be under the car. Then when he crawled down into the ditch, he could see my arm dangling over the side of the car, but there still was no answer when he spoke to me.

Troy said there was no way to get me out of the ditch until the car could be moved in some way, so he hitched the two mules to one of the wheels and turned the car on its side. He said both of us were a muddy mess by that time, and, since it was dark by then, he could not even see my face. He knew I was still alive, even though I was unconscious, because I was breathing. He got the car uprighted on its wheels, put me on the back seat, and the two mules pulled it about a hundred yards up the road to his house.

He said he and his wife decided the best thing to do was to carry me inside the house, take off my muddy clothes, wash me, and put me to bed until morning. The nearest doctor was eleven miles away in Clarksdale and there was no way to telephone.

After I had been washed and put into bed, Troy told me, he and his wife felt my arms and legs and ribs until they were confident that I had no broken bones. There were only two rooms in the house and, since I was in one of the only two beds, the children slept in the other one and he and Mandy took turns sleeping on a quilt in the kitchen. Keeping the lamp burning all night, one of them sat beside the bed and kept watch over me until daybreak.

It was about nine o'clock that morning when I finally woke up and saw them for the first time.

They brought me a plate of scrambled eggs and a lot of bacon and a baking pan of Mandy's hot biscuits, but my head was aching so much that I could eat very little, and I told Troy I wanted to leave and get back to Millington as soon as I could. My left arm was still numb and dangling at my side, and, even if I had been able to use it, the automobile was in no condition to be driven. The front axle was sprung, one of the wheels had fallen off, and all the gasoline and oil had leaked out while the car was upside down in the ditch.

Troy told me that a passenger train would be going from Clarksdale to Memphis in the afternoon and that if we went to Coahoma, two miles up the road, the station agent would flag it down for a passenger. Assuring me that he would take good care of the car and not let anybody touch it until it was sent for, Troy hitched the two mules to the wagon and we drove up the road to Coahoma.

Along the way I told Troy about Bisco in Middle Georgia and how we had been playmates when we were very young and that when I woke up that morning I was sure I was in Bisco's house and that he and Mandy were Bisco's parents. I had hoped Troy would say that he or his wife were kin to Bisco, or at least knew him, but he said all their relatives lived in Mississippi and that he had never known anybody from Georgia. However, he did say that he was proud to be somebody who reminded me of a fine fellow like Bisco and he hoped that someday Bisco and I would come back together to visit so all of us could have a big all-day reunion with Mandy cooking us one of her fried chicken dinners.

When we were within sight of Coahoma, I began wondering how I could repay Troy for everything he had done for me from the time he found me under the car in the ditch until he put me on the train to Memphis. By that time I was beginning to realize that I might have drowned in the rising water in the ditch if Troy had not found me in time to save my life. I still had ten dollars the YMCA secretary had given me for expenses and a few dollars of my own, but I did not know how much the train ticket would cost.

When we got to the railroad station in Coahoma, I bought a ticket only as far as Memphis, and not all the way to Millington, since it would cost less and I knew I could get a free ride in an army truck from Memphis to Millington.

After paying for the ticket, I had almost ten dollars left and I gave all of it to Troy. He protested and tried to make me take it back, saying that everything he had done was a favor and he did not want pay for being friendly. He said there was so much unfriendliness in the world that it made him feel proud to have a chance to do a favor for a white man.

The train stopped at the station only long enough for me to get aboard. Standing on the steps of the coach as the train began to move, I realized it was unlikely that I would ever see Troy again and it reminded me of the last time I had seen Bisco. Looking backward from the steps, I could see Troy waving to me until the train went out of sight around a curve.

Late that night in Millington I told the YMCA secretary what had happened to his car, though quickly assuring him that it would be safe at Troy's house until it could be towed back to Clarksdale for repairs.

Frowning and shaking his head, the secretary was silent for several moments. Presently he said that he should have listened to his wife and left the automobile where it was in Clarksdale. When he asked me if I had been hurt when the car turned over, I told him that my arm was sore and that I still had a headache. After that he asked how his wife was when I saw her. I told him that she had said she was lonely in Clarksdale and wanted to come to Millington.

He looked at me with a quick glance and said that I had better get my head examined. Then, as he walked away, he told me that he wanted me to be ready to drive him to Memphis in the YMCA staff car on Friday afternoon for the week end.

13

The Negro student of the nineteen-sixties in Bisco Country has come of age undaunted by a racial heritage of fear, docility, and subservience. Even though he is still in high school or junior college, and one of the many thousands unlikely to have the opportunity to study at a major university in the South, education has already inspired him with a desire for the freedom of conduct and expression his parents and grandparents never knew.

Now for the first time the Negro student in Arkansas or elsewhere in the Deep South has the courage to rebel openly against the social and economic restrictions that have been imposed upon his race for the past two centuries. And like students everywhere in the contemporary world, he does not hesitate to reject the reactionary principles of the established order when they attempt to suppress the progressive ideals of youth.

All traditions cling tenaciously to the past, and racial traditions in particular are deeply rooted in the white man's South. As most Negro students know, they have a long way to go before they will be able to cross the long-established color lines and succeed in abolishing racial discrimination and placing it in a chapter of history. They are learning that the passage of law granting civil rights is one thing and that the banishment of prejudice is something else.

What inspires students everywhere is the universal human desire for freedom. In this new era of total emancipation in America, education is providing Negro youth with the promise of freedom as well as the vision to see it within reach. It is no wonder, then, that Negro students are rapidly acquiring the courage to put in their claim for social freedom as well as civil freedom.

The trouble is, though, that claiming a right, or making a demand for it, has not always been enough. Resorting to violence and revolt has often been the only means of striving to gain an idealistic aim; however, this is essentially an appeal to public opinion, which is a potent force in a democracy and is capable of being more effective than a display of might. This is why the act of integrating a restaurant and sitting at a lunch counter is merely a token demonstration against discrimination. The ultimate success of desegregation will be decreed not by law but by the sympathy and humanity of people.

What the serious Negro student has always hoped to accomplish by go-ins and stand-ins and sit-ins was much more than having the right to order a sandwich from a white waitress in a public place and to eat it in a white man's presence. His real objective is to gain the right—even at the cost of civil disobedience if necessary—to have the same opportunity as a white student to study law or economics or medicine or engineering at the university of his choice. Like everybody else, he knows that the policy of avowed segregationists in the Deep South to provide equal, but separate, educational institutions for Negro and white has been as discriminatory and undemocratic in fact as the intent is in purpose.

The ambition of the eighteen-year-old Negro high school senior in Little Rock is to be a chemical engineer. He is an A-student in chemistry and physics at a Negro high school and he would like to attend the state university and study for advanced degrees in industrial engineering. There is no likelihood now of his being admitted to the state university when he graduates from high school. When the time comes that he would be admitted, his school days will be too far behind him and he will have become an involuntary dropout.

I don't know what's going to happen to me. I could never get enough money to go North to a good university. The Negro colleges in Arkansas don't offer the advanced courses I want to take. My folks don't have the money to send me out of the state where tuition would be very high. But if I could go to the state university here, I'd manage by working at some kind of job. I like experimenting in chemistry and working with oil and pulp to find some new synthetics.

If I could keep on, maybe I'd discover something that's never been done before—just like some people have done by experimenting with pines and peanuts and such things. That takes a lot of study, though, and better laboratories than we've got at high school. Maybe someday they'll open up the state university for everybody, but right now it looks like it'll be too late for me.

I've applied for scholarships at a lot of universities in the North. So far nothing's happened. I'm still hoping, though. I guess they get a lot of applications from people like me down here, and they can't help everybody. If I'm lucky, I might get one. But if I don't get a scholarship, I'll try to think of something else to do about it. I don't want to spend my life swabbing toilets and washrooms like my daddy does.

We do a lot of talking at school about segregation and such things, but there's not much new to be said about it—unless Dick Gregory says something funny. You learn more about that by looking around and seeing how it is in Little Rock. Everything's divided right down the middle—black and white, Negro and white, colored and white, nigger and white.

You can't do this and you can't do that. Watch your talk and watch your step. Get going, nigger. That's what the young white boys say. My folks are used to it. They've lived with it all their lives—forty years or more. My dad's always telling me to watch out and take care and keep my mouth shut and stay out of trouble. My mother's the same way—she's scared to death of white people.

I'm not exactly scared. I just don't like it. That's all. It doesn't seem right—having to keep from doing something or going somewhere because some white people don't want you to. I'm not going to do something wrong when it's against the law. I know better than that. But the way it is, there're a lot of things a colored boy will get in trouble about. A white man will give you a shove for nothing at all. Even if you don't shove back, they'll claim it's a scuffle and then you're taken off to jail for disturbing the peace.

That's what I don't like about the way Negroes are treated. Whites know how to get around the civil rights law. You can be walking along the street where it's crowded and watching your step all the way. Then if you accidentally get pushed against a white man it can be real bad trouble even if it wasn't your fault. And if he's a mean white—even if you apologize and say you're sorry—colored can get knocked down or shot at for as little as that.

I don't have hard feelings toward all white people. I wouldn't know what to hate them about—except the mean ones. Most of them are richer than the colored and a lot of them have fine cars and live in big houses. But that's no reason to hate them—I'd have a fine car and a big house myself if I could. And there are a lot of colored better off than poor whites. The way I see it, that sort of evens things up fifty-fifty. And I don't hate them because they have white skin and I've got black skin. That makes no more difference to me than if they're Methodist and I'm Baptist or something.

The one kind of white man I don't like is the one who'll cheat you—and there're plenty of those. They're the ones who make a big living by cheating the colored. Some of them are the bill collectors who come around once a week to collect installment payments for something that's been bought on time—like a TV or a washing machine or some furniture. Some of the other cheating kind are the salesmen who go house-to-house selling something that's going to be shoddy even if they never come back and deliver it after collecting the down payment. Those cheating whites have all kind of tricks. They're the whites you've got to watch out for.

Some of the installment collectors will claim you're two weeks behind in payments and say they'll call the police if you don't pay double. I've seen some of them pull back their coats and show a pistol if you don't give them the money in a hurry.

The cheating salesmen will show samples and take orders for what they're selling and collect a dollar or more down payment and then never deliver what they've promised. They leave town and never come back again and you can't call the police and have them arrested for cheating or get your money back.

I've never been up North and I don't know what it's like up there. I've heard a lot of talk about it, though, and some will say Negroes are better off living in Chicago or St. Louis and others will say that's no different than right here in Little Rock. They say the pay is better up there and you can eat better and have finer clothes. Others will say Negroes have to live in a certain part of town just like here and pay lots more rent, too. If that's true, I don't see much difference.

As much as I know about it, being a Negro is just about the same no matter where you live. The way it is now the whites are going to try to boss you wherever you are.

What I want to do is get a good education so I can be my own boss. That's the only way a Negro can get what he wants. The trouble right now is that I don't know how I'm going to get more education after I finish high school.

I've never been mixed up in any of the fights a crowd of white boys will come around and start. I'm not scared of them and I'll fist-fight if I have to, but I'm not going to get out there in the street and throw rocks and swing bicycle chains. I've got something better to do. Colored students ought to be spending their time studying all they can so they can get good jobs when they leave school. Otherwise, if they don't watch out, they'll end up cleaning washrooms and hauling garbage and shining shoes for white people for the rest of their lives.

That's one thing you can say for me. I'm not going to be satisfied hiring out like that. I don't know yet how I'm going to make my way like I want to, but I'm going to get started by getting the best education I can somehow or other. That's something I've promised myself. I might not get very high up, but I sure won't be down at the bottom of things.

It's what I've been saying that I've got against people who come around and say Negroes ought to get out and spend their time spiting whites and do everything they can to make the whites suffer. I've heard some of them say spit on white people and rob them and knife them. They've got clubs just to do that.

That makes no sense to me. If Negro students spend their time trying to harm white people in some way, they're not helping themselves at all. That'd be wasting the time they could be educating themselves so they could get some of the good jobs the white people have the first call on now.

My dad says voting is going to make a big difference about things before long. He says when the colored start doing that the way they should, there'll be a lot of changes made. That makes more sense to me than joining the white-hating clubs.

That's why you won't see me spitting on white people and carrying a gun or pulling a knife. I'm going to be studying somewhere. Right now I don't know how I'm going to do it, but I'll find a way somehow.

14

The Gumbo Negroes of Southern Arkansas have been in the United States just as long as the Gullahs of South Carolina, the Geechees of Georgia, and the Guineas of Alabama and Mississippi.

However, it was the fate of the Gumboes to be the first among Negro Americans to be displaced as farm laborers by cotton harvesting machines. This is a distinction thrust upon the Gumboes on Delta plantations in Arkansas with as little regard for their welfare as the first Africans received when they were shackled, shipped across the Atlantic and sold into lifetime slavery.

In origin, Gumboes were the Angola slaves sold at auction in New Orleans during the late seventeen-hundreds and early eighteen-hundreds. They were given their new-world name for being identified with

okra, called gumbo in their native Bantu language
when it was mixed with other ingredients for a meal,
and the seedpods of which had been their bedding
and food aboard slave ships.

When bought by plantation owners—and taking
their remaining okra seedpods with them—the Gumboes were sent to Eastern Louisiana and Southern
Arkansas to clear the land of trees and raise cotton
in the fertile alluvial soil of the flood plains of the
Mississippi River.

The word gumbo probably would not have survived and become permanently established in the
American language if the female Angola slaves had
not been kept in New Orleans by the French as con-
cubines and if the males on the plantations had not
been provided with female Ouachita Indians for
sexual partners.

As time went on, the mulatto male offspring were
sent from New Orleans to the plantations—in quick
progression the female becoming quadroon and octoroon—and the planters, using cloth and trinkets as
inducements, lured females of the Ouachita Indians
to the plantations to become child-bearing.

As the result of this African-French-Indian fusion,
gumbo became the popular descriptive term for anything or anybody produced by a mixture—soup, soil,
vegetation and African, French, Indian.

Now, in the nineteen-sixties, descendants of the
Gumbo slaves, their bright tan coloring and sharply-
profiled Gallic faces distinguishing them from other

Negro Americans, are being displaced by farm machinery and sent into exile. From the point of view of agricultural economists, they are obsolete labor units without salvage value. Picking cotton by hand on the delta farms of Arkansas nowadays would be as economically antiquated as mowing a six-hundred-forty-acre section of Nebraska wheat with a sickle.

Being sent into exile from a Southern Arkansas cotton farm means, to many Negroes, becoming a wandering refugee in his own native America. After having been dispossessed and evicted from his two-room tenant-farm homeplace, which was usually his birthplace as well, an elderly Negro is a social and economic outcast with no place to go and without the likelihood of being able to earn an adequate living. Moreover, having been a farm laborer all his life and consequently not eligible for social security, he will not receive benefit payments when he is sixty-five and older.

But even this is not always the ultimate fate of a social and economic outcast. Many of the smaller towns in isolated parts of the cotton belt have devised insidiously authoritative means of preventing a farm-exiled Negro family from living within corporate limits and thereby becoming eligible for local welfare aid of a few dollars a month. When this takes place, families are ordered, and forced by police intimidation or edict, to keep moving and go somewhere else.

The usual result of being forced by small-town

command to keep moving is that such unwanted Negro families eventually find themselves crowded into shacks and hovels in the already over-crowded segregated sections of Pine Bluff and Little Rock. The younger Negroes often go to Chicago and Detroit in search of work and a better place to live. The elderly exiles stay behind and pass their remaining years in poverty and squalor and hopelessness.

The tall, thin, bright-brown Gumbo with a characteristic African-French-Indian facial profile and straight black hair turning gray is sixty-six years old. Usually he has a job for two or three days a week working as yardboy. When he works, he is paid forty cents an hour for a full day mowing grass, cultivating flowers, trimming hedges, and raking leaves. He said he pays four dollars a week to rent the house where he and his wife live in the swampy lowland Negro section of Pine Bluff.

I don't mind telling about myself. I aint got a thing to be ashamed of. I worked hard all my life and I'm proud of it. I went to work on a cotton plantation about thirty miles down south of here when I was ten or eleven years old. I stayed right there on that same plantation all my life up to a little more than a year ago when I was getting close to sixty-five.

That's when the white man said I'd got too old and slowed down to do much good for him. He told me and my wife to pick up and leave. I wasn't looking to hear him say a thing like that. It was the worst surprise I ever had in all my life. I'd put in the past fifty-some years working the cotton for the white man and his daddy before him and I sure hated hearing him tell me I couldn't stay no longer and had to go off somewhere else.

My folks lived on that same plantation down there all their lifetime, too. It was the only homeplace me and them ever had. My wife was born down there, too, and me and her had just one daughter only. She got married to a Sanctified traveling preacher who came by from over across the Big River and stopped and preached once and took up a collection and then they went traveling off to California. I aint seen her since and don't reckon I never will again.

That preacher said he'd been born 'way back in Georgia somewhere and grew up mostly in Alabama and Mississippi where his daddy was a sometime sawmill man. His name was Henry, but he never did say what his daddy's name was and I don't know if it was Bisco or Frisco or anything like that. Anyhow, he was a big handsome man even if he was a poor-mouth Sanctified preacher.

Like I was saying, I was a pretty good cotton hand down there on the plantation. And the white man used to say so, too, up to the time when he changed his mind about it one day. I didn't know things went wrong somehow until he came up and started complaining about how slow I was doing the picking. My old hands had got a little stiff in the joints and I just couldn't make my old fingers move quick enough to pick cotton faster no matter how hard I tried. But the white man said that was nothing but my own fault and none of his.

The white man said everybody else on the place but me was picking up to four hundred pounds a day and I was having a hard time getting up to near two hundred. My wife tried her best to help me out, but her back's been bad a long time and she couldn't stoop over enough to do much good. I just couldn't never get much picked over two hundred even when she helped out the best she could.

The white man'd already bought two cotton picking machines and was fixing to get two more. I asked him please let me change over to running a machine picker in the field for him instead of hand picking. But he said I was past sixty and too old to learn how to run the machine good enough. He put the young boys to running the machine pickers and told me I was so old I'd be better off quitting and going somewhere to retire, anyhow.

That was when the white man said times has changed a lot and he wanted me to go off somewhere else and look after myself the best I could from then on. He said I was a heap better off than the mules he got rid of when he bought the picking machines. He didn't have to tell me how he figured that. He sold those mules to the dog food factory. They hit those mules on the head with a sledge hammer and hauled them off on a truck one on top of the other. It was a sad sight to see those good old mules end up like that. I'd been feeding them and treating them for

colic and plowing them for I don't know how long.
You get to know mules by name when you do that,
and they know you, too. Don't think they don't. It's
just like being people together.

I begged about it, but the white man wouldn't
even let me keep on living on the place and chop
cotton for him. He said he could get all the Mexicans
he needed at cotton-chopping time and pay them
sixty cents an hour and not have to provide houses
for them because they could sleep in the barn and
he could get rid of them by cutting off their pay the
same sundown the chopping was finished. I couldn't
never figure why the Mexicans got paid sixty cents
an hour for doing the same work the colored was paid
thirty cents for. The white man said it was the government law, but it didn't sound fair and square for
the government to do a thing like that.

Anyhow, I felt real sorry for those Mexican folks.
They didn't even know what the word was for what
they was doing none of the time. They'd have to
point at something like when they wanted a drink of
water or a match to light up their tobacco.

When the white man said for me to pick up and
go, I told him I didn't have a single dollar to my
name to live on after that. He said that wasn't no
fault of his. He said he wasn't God Almighty and
didn't have nothing to do with the way things was
in the world. He told me to pray about it and maybe
I'd get some advice that way. I'm a religious man,
but I never heard of the Good Lord telling anybody

where to go to look to find money. Even the preachers can't get it that way.

I thought sure he'd let me and my wife stay on the place till we died, but he wouldn't pay attention to no talk like that. He said he was going to burn down my old house because it stood in the way of the machines and slowed work.

Like everybody knows, a colored man can't just stand there keeping on begging like that with a white man. A white man is liable to get mad at you and no telling what'd happen to you. I've seen bad things happen too many times in my life and I don't want none of that kind of trouble. Not at my age, I don't.

The last thing I spoke to the white man was I felt mighty sad leaving the plantation after being born on it and living and working down there on it for him and his daddy all my life since I was ten or eleven years old. That's all I could say. There wasn't nothing else I could think of to tell him that he'd be apt to listen to.

He told me he'd let one of the young colored boys take me and my wife in a truck to Pine Bluff or anywhere else we wanted to go just so it wasn't no farther off than Pine Bluff. He told me I could take the furniture and anything else that belonged to me and my wife. Then he gave me ten dollars of his own money out of his pocket and walked off. He walked off so quick I never got a chance to thank him for the money or nothing like that.

There's been some other old folks like me and my wife who'd been sent off the plantations and come to Pine Bluff when the white man said he didn't need none of us no more, but I didn't know how to locate none of them in such a big city where everybody was a stranger to me. When me and my wife got here to Pine Bluff in the truck, the best I could do was look for a friendly man and ask him please let me unload the furniture in his front yard. I had to do something like that quick because the boy driving the truck said he'd been warned to unload and hurry back to the plantation before dark and he was scared not to.

There wasn't much furniture on the truck—only some chairs and kitchen table and my wife's old sewing machine and things like that. But when it was all piled up on that truck with the bedstead on top, people seeing us drive around looking for a place to stay must've thought a big flood was on the way and time for everybody to find a place safe from the high water.

Anyhow, I don't know what I'd done if I hadn't come across a friendly colored man who took pity on me. He let me and my wife unload the furniture in his front yard and said we could put some quilts down and sleep on his front porch. We stayed there four days cooking on his cookstove and sleeping on his porch before I could locate a house to move to and rent for four dollars.

The big trouble about that was the rats. I'm used to some rats, but not like the big fat ones that come out at night here in Pine Bluff and crawl all over you when you're trying to sleep like they own the whole world. Country rats don't bother me none, but these city rats sure make me nervous.

My big worry besides the rats is making a living, because I'm getting old fast. Not many white folks want to hire an old man like me. They say the young colored boys work harder and faster for the same pay. But I've just got to make a living somehow if I can't get the social security. I've been told about state welfare pay, but that don't amount to much, nohow.

The way it's been, I've had about twenty or more yardboy jobs in nearly a year and a half and can't find a steady job to save my life. I work two or three days in a week sometimes and then get paid off and told not to come back no more after that. Then I have to go looking for another yardboy job somewhere in town. The longest lasting job I had was three weeks. And that only added up to six whole pay-days of work.

I know I do good yard work. People tell me so, too. But somehow they just don't want me working steady for them. I've asked some of the white people why they had to let me go. One of them told me it was some kind of trouble about the social security. A white lady said if I worked steady all the time for her, and kept it up for two or three months she'd have to pay out extra money to the government for the social security. She said she'd rather hire a different yardboy every two weeks or so and not pay the social security money.

That's something else that bothers me all the time. If anybody needs the social security, it sure is me. But I just can't find a way to get connected with it so I can draw some of the welfare money. Looks like everybody else except me is connected with it somehow, because just about everybody I work for says they has to deduct about a dollar from my pay for the tax. It's hard on me to lose a dollar out of my pay like that nearly every week and never get none of it back.

I don't like to come right out in the open and say some white people do something wrong. I wasn't raised to talk like that. But if it aint wrong it still don't look exactly right. I went to the social security place not long ago and asked the people down there when I would be due to get some government security money because I was already past sixty-five. I didn't expect it to amount to much but I sure thought I'd get something. They said it'd likely be nothing at all because I wasn't covered with it.

I told those people I'd worked on the plantation all my life up to a year or more ago and had been doing yard work in Pine Bluff for the past year and that sometimes when I got paid off I was short a whole dollar they told me was the deduct to pay the tax.

But the people at the social security place said the whole time I was working at farm work on the plantation didn't count none and the deducts from yard-boy pay don't mean nothing at all because I didn't work steady for the same people long enough at a time to count. They told me I ought to keep people from making the deducts till I got a steady job and worked at the same place three or four months. That's what they said exactly. But they don't know how hard it is for an old colored man like me to speak up and tell white folks the right thing they ought to do.

If I was a lot younger, I'd start right in and say to the white people they ought to pay me all the money when I do work for them and don't hold some back and call it deduct for the social security for me that aint. I hear the young colored people talk like that, but I'm an old-timey darky and I just can't make myself say it at my age.

The benefit security pay is the big thing I want to get hold of. If they'd put that in the civil rights, I'd sure have something to be thankful about. And then while they're about it, I wish they'd put something in the law about those rats down there where all us colored live. My feet stick out the end of the bed because it's shorter than me and hardly a night goes by when I don't get a rat bite on one or both my big toes. I can put up with a lot of hardship, but I just can't get used to those rats that come out from some-where in the dark of night.

15

For more than a century and a half the Deep South was wholly dependent upon the servitude and muscle of the Negro to do its work and produce its wealth. Cotton farming, the principal source of wealth for the white Southern landowner, could not have prospered without the labor of the Gullah, Geechee, Guinea, and Gumbo. But now times have changed and mechanized agriculture is replacing human muscles with tractors, harvesters, and combines.

There are already many regions in the agricultural South where the Negro laborer is no longer useful as a worker and, as it follows, is no longer wanted as a citizen. Among these regions—other than the mechanized cotton belt—is the Grand Prairie of Eastern Arkansas. This is one place in Bisco Country where cotton, because of unsuitable soil, will not grow and thrive; now it is also hostile ground for the Negro American.

The Grand Prairie is a small empire in the bayou region between the Mississippi and Arkansas rivers that has produced more rice during the past fifty years than any other region in the United States. Few Americans rely upon rice as a basic food, but beer drinkers would go thirsty and put up a loud clamor if brewers could not have an ample supply of it.

The three necessary natural elements for the production of rice—thin soil on hardpan base, abundant water, and sub-tropical climate—have always been present in this region of Arkansas. And now rice farming on the Grand Prairie has become the most completely mechanized of all agricultural operations in the nation. This combination of natural circumstances and perfected technology has made the production of rice relatively effortless, highly profitable, and no longer dependent upon the use of human labor.

Rice paddies on the Grand Prairie are contoured and terraced by levee machines; flooding and irrigation are electronically timed and controlled; seeding and fertilizing are done by airplanes; and the largest combines that have yet been devised for such agricultural purposes harvest the rice crop. Such specialized machinery and techniques require skilled operators, and the stoop-labor Negro was not one of those privileged to receive the essential training in a white man's country. Like the mules that were no longer useful and were sold to the dog food cannery, the Negro laborers too were sent to their destiny elsewhere.

The wealthy owner of nearly five hundred acres of riceland paddies on the Grand Prairie between Stuttgart and DeWitt is a soft-spoken, friendly-mannered, white Protestant Southerner in his fifties. He was born in Arkansas, he was educated in Arkansas, he inherited the land from his father, he is untraveled beyond the Mid-South, he is fiercely imbued with the Southerner's hatred of the Negro, and he has been a rice grower for thirty years. During the first twenty years, all the work of raising rice was done by mules and Negroes; now neither a mule nor a Negro remains on the farm.

Nowadays the owner employs a land-leveling company to terrace his paddies; he uses an aerial farming service to seed and fertilize; and he contracts with still another company to harvest with combines. Each third year, as scientific rice growers do, he leases his flooded paddies in a rotation of acreage to a commercial fish hatchery for the purpose of restoring fertility to the soil. Such expert management of rice farms is not unusual on the Grand Prairie. After all, the owner is not a mere dirt farmer; he is an efficient businessman in stylish country clothing.

I'll tell you exactly how it is, he said. We don't need niggers around here. We finished using them a long time ago when we changed over from mules to machines. The niggers know it, too. They've gone away and won't never come back. That's why you don't see their black asses around shacks on rice farms like you still do in some parts of the cotton country in Arkansas.

I bulldozed some of their stinking shacks and set fire to the rest of them when I stopped hiring niggers about five years ago and told them to pick up and get the hell off my land. Some of the old niggers put on a pitiful face and said they didn't have nowhere to go. I told them I didn't give a good God damn where they went and the country would be better off if they went to hell or back to Africa. You have to talk like that to niggers to get any sense through their thick black skulls.

Some of the younger niggers tried to get me to let them learn tractor driving, but I wouldn't listen to that, neither. You let fucking niggers stay on your place and before you know it every one of them has a sackful of bastard kids, maybe eight or ten or more, and that means you'd have to pay more taxes to build their schools and hire their teachers. When I pay school taxes, I want my money to go to educate white children—not black-assed niggers. And that's how it worked out. We got rid of them and kept our school taxes down at the same time.

I don't know where all of them went when they left here. They just disappeared. Went somewhere out of sight. Thank God. That's why we've got a lower percentage of niggers in our county than you'll find anywhere in Arkansas. The few niggers left here in the county now are no more than ten or fifteen per cent of the whole population. That's good. It's a damn good showing when you think that nearly everywhere else in Arkansas the black bastards are fifty per cent or more.

You'll find a few of them working around the rice mills in Stuttgart doing the heavy work and others will be janitoring and hauling garbage. We need a few to stay and do that kind of work. I wouldn't want to see a white man shoveling garbage and cleaning toilet stools. That's nigger-work. The same about cooking and house-cleaning, too. We couldn't get along without enough nigger women to do that for us.

What happened to most of the dinges who left the rice farms was that they went to Little Rock and Memphis and somewhere up North. It's hard on the white people in Little Rock and Memphis, but I'm glad a lot of them went up North and gave the bleeding-hearts up there a whopping big dose of what they've been begging for.

We never had Georgia niggers living here. When we needed niggers on the Grand Prairie in the old days—hell, we raised our own. That was no trouble—we had plenty of fucking niggers around here for that. And that's why we didn't need to get them from Georgia. I know all about those Georgia niggers—most of them are half-assed whites and we don't want them coming to Arkansas and stirring up our niggers with wrong notions. Whenever I saw one from Georgia or Alabama, I'd tell him to go back where he came from or else keep on moving to Texas. I dont know if one of them was named Bisco or not. I never heard that name for a nigger, but it sounds like one of those half-assed whites from Georgia.

They talk real big up North about segregation and discrimination down here and now we'll see how smart they are about handling niggers. They've been doing their fault-finding up North for a long time and now we can sit back and watch the Yankees squirm and run for cover and holler for help.

I'll pass the hat any day, and match anybody's money with my own, to buy bus tickets for any nigger and his wife and ten bastard kids to go North and live with the Yankees. That's a standing offer with me and I'm always glad when I have a chance to do it.

I'll tell you why it makes sense to do that. This country around here is just as safe to live in now as it is pretty. There's nothing to be scared of, day or night, like it is where the niggers live by the thousands in the big cities and where they'll knife a white man for his money and get their hands on a white woman for rape. You can go out after dark here and think nothing of it. There's no black bastards prowling around at night now to hit you on the head or stick a knife in you. Even a white woman without her titty-bags on is safe to go where she pleases day or night anywhere on the Grand Prairie and not get stripped naked and thrown down and nigger-raped.

I dare the Yankees to make a claim like that and try to prove it.

Everybody knows what happens up North all the time where a lot of niggers went. You read about it in the papers and hear about it on television. And I'll bet you that's only the half of it. Robbing, killing, raping, and everything else you can think of. But even that's only the beginning. Just wait a while. It's going to get a hell of a lot worse all over the country. And a lot of people are going to get hurt—if not killed. The only way to stop it now is for the nigger-lovers to wake up and find out it's this thing about civil rights that's the cause of it.

The only civil rights the niggers ought to have is what they already had—and that was too many for them. They could ride on the highways and watch the same television shows the white people did and buy what they wanted in the stores. But when the law tells them they can live in any part of town they please and eat in the same restaurants you do—then that's encouraging them. And that's what they want. Encouragement. You give them an inch of that and they'll stop at nothing. They'll claim it's discrimination unless they can get white women next. I know what I'm talking about. I wasn't born and raised in Arkansas for nothing.

None of this trouble would've started in the first place if people up North had had the sense to leave well enough alone. But no—they came down South to Little Rock and New Orleans and Birmingham and other big cities and started talking like a bunch of damn fools about segregation and discrimination and civil rights. The whole country was getting along fine up to then. We had the niggers in their place all over the South and they damn-well stayed in it.

But those bleeding-heart Yankees from the North—and even some from Washington, too—started stirring up trouble by telling the niggers they ought to have more civil rights. That's when the niggers started thinking they were as good as white people. So it wasn't long till they claimed they had to have equal rights in everything. They started out wanting to send their black-assed kids to white schools and eating in white restaurants. But that was only the beginning and there's no end to what they'll try to get after this.

Now the Yankees up North are getting a whopping big dose of their own medicine and it's gagging them in the gullet. While they're trying to puke it out, it makes them realize they don't want to associate with niggers up there no more than we do down here. That's why they are wishing to God they'd never started this thing.

All right. So now they've got the civil rights law. But before this thing started, the niggers were peaceful and quiet and satisfied. They didn't expect no more than what they already had. Now there's no end to what they'll try to do from now on. They already talk like they think they can take over the whole country and run it as they God damn please.

If it keeps on, the next thing'll be that they'll say they want a law passed that'll make it a crime for white whores not to give them equal rights.

The government in Washington can pass all the laws they want and print them in letters a foot high and nail them to every God damn telephone pole in Arkansas, but nigger-loving laws won't make us change our ways of handling them. We've got our own way of doing things. You'll never find me living in a house next to niggers shitting and pissing all around the place. If that's what the Yankee nigger-lovers want, they can have it, but by God nobody's going to make me put up with all that nigger stink. Before I'd put up with it, I'd set fire to their house or dynamite it to-hell-and-gone.

It sure was a lucky thing for us that we got rid of the niggers on the Grand Prairie long before this trouble started. The way it is now, we can feel sorry for the Yankees in the North and be glad about our own selves at the same time. It's a God damn pity about the Yankees, but they asked for it and now they're stuck with it.

16

The town of Bastrop has been built on a gritty hummock that rises a few feet above the perennial green flatland of delta grass in Northeast Louisiana.

The courthouse square is Bastrop's principal business district and, like small-town county seats throughout Bisco Country, it is surrounded by the usual predominance of fifty-dollar loan company offices, cubbyholes of ubiquitous white-shirted lawyers, drug stores selling lawn furniture and little red tricycles, and variety shops with fly-specked window displays of women's twenty-nine-cent pink rayon panties.

This is where white merchants solicit the Negro's dollar, and then, as soon as it is in hand, and with the practiced brusqueness of a practical whore, send him back to confinement in his segregated shantytown until he earns another dollar to spend.

Beyond the courthouse square and along its tree-shaded, white-skin residential streets, Bastrop is still not unlike many other towns in the Deep South where the white half of nine or ten thousand people live, work, and conform to the century-old social, religious, and political customs of the community.

As elsewhere from South Carolina to Louisiana, absolute white skin and either a pretense of wealth or assumed aristocratic ancestry are necessary prerequisites in Bastrop for acceptable economic status and social standing. Likewise, unfailing church attendance and unwavering loyalty to the entrenched political machine are required to be posted as public records before full citizenship is granted. Non-conformists and other dissidents in Bastrop quickly find out that they have the choice of doing either of two things—conform or suffer social and economic boycott.

It was Bastrop's fate in its beginning to be geographically isolated in a hip pocket of Louisiana. Consequently, it is its misfortune to have been culturally by-passed since its days of plantation glory in the nineteenth century. The town's few paved roads come from the backwoods of Southern Arkansas and its local roads disappear somewhere in the swamps between the Mississippi and Ouachita rivers. The one access the town has to the rest of the world is a forty-mile highway to Monroe, the only place within nearly a hundred miles that has a city-size population.

However, Bastrop does continue to exist and pros-

per with good reason. It is in the center of an extensive region rich in cotton, timber, cattle, and
chemical industry and it is populated by an abundant supply of thirty-cent-an-hour and fifteen-dollar-
a-week Gumbo Negro laborers. With such a combination of wealth-producing natural and human
resources, it is as content now as it was a century ago
to be geographically remote and culturally isolated in
America.

Contentment is likely to continue among Bastrop's
cotton planters, timbermen, and cattlemen as long as
the Negro laborer can be kept under social, economic,
and political domination—which even in the nineteen-
sixties means keeping the Negro in his place—and as
long as ingenious means can be devised to perpetuate sub-standard wage scales.

All this is a familiar way of life to many Southerners of both races who live in the states bordering
the Mississippi River from Memphis to New Orleans.
However, the white Northerner, and particularly the
New Englander, who moves to this region of the
Deep South to work as a technician or engineer or
supervisor in an industrial plant often finds it dif-
ficult, if not impossible, to condone expressions of
racial hatred and acts of spite. Usually, Northerners
soon discover that the famed Southern hospitality so
graciously offered guests at the front door can be
transformed immediately afterward into tirades of
ruthless abuse and intimidation forced upon Negro
servants at the back door.

The forty-year-old college-educated wife of a petroleum engineer had lived in Bastrop with her husband and three children for nearly two years. They had always lived in New England before moving to Louisiana and she and her husband had never been able to afford to employ a servant until they came to Bastrop. Her husband's increase in salary, and the prevailing low wages for servants in Bastrop, had made it possible for them to employ a full-time Negro maid.

The first time I realized something was wrong was about a year ago, she said. My husband and I had made many friends in town and I knew some of our closest neighbors very well by then. It was one morning soon after breakfast when one of the neighbors came to the door and said she and another neighbor were having coffee at her house and they wanted me to join them. I was pleased to be invited and of course I went.

The three of us talked casually about nothing in particular for about five minutes while we were drinking coffee. Then one of the women suddenly spoke in a sharp tone of voice and said she and several other women on our street were having trouble with their maids and that it was all my fault. I was so taken by surprise that I thought she was joking and I laughed.

There was a long silence in the room and I could see the tense expressions of anger on their faces. Realizing then how serious they were, I asked what

I had done to cause any trouble. Asking that one question was the only chance I had to speak again for what seemed like a full half-hour. They were so angry that both of them were trying to talk at once during most of the time.

Even so, it didn't take long to find out why they were so angry and upset. I had been in the habit of giving our Negro maid a little extra money whenever my husband and I had guests for dinner. Kathy's salary of fifteen dollars a week was exactly the same as the other full-time maids in town received, but I just could not let her work several hours longer than usual at night without paying her extra for it. And even when we had just a few people come for cocktails, I always gave Kathy something extra then, too.

Kathy had never complained about the salary we paid her, and I'd been careful to find out what the prevailing wages were before I offered her the job, but the pay was so small for the work she did—and for the long hours, too—that I was ashamed to pay her so little. I suppose you could say my husband and I wanted to conform to local customs because we intended to live here for a long time.

Anyway, I was always glad when we invited guests to dinner or cocktails and had a good reason to give her a few dollars extra to make up for the small salary.

Then, besides that, I've always had a weakness for wanting to make small gifts to people I knew well, and so once in a while I'd buy something at a store that I knew Kathy wanted or actually needed. She has five children and her husband is a janitor who also makes only fifteen dollars a week. The gifts never cost more than two or three dollars, but I know they were worth many times that much to her.

What had happened was that some of the Negro maids who worked for our neighbors found out that I was giving Kathy something extra now and then, as well as occasional gifts, in addition to her salary. I couldn't blame Kathy for talking about it and I couldn't blame the other maids, either, for wanting some extra pay when they had to work longer than eight or nine hours.

I'd supposed that everybody would feel obligated to pay a servant something extra for working as late as midnight, after working all day, too. I was so upset that morning when those two women talked the way they did that I told them that anybody who'd make a Negro maid work much longer than her usual hours, and then not pay her something in addition, should not be permitted to have a servant. I was damn mad about it.

I don't know what else I said that morning, because I was so upset I might've said anything. Whatever it was I did say, it must've been to the point, because neither of those two women has spoken to me or invited me to her house since. That means I'm on their outcast list and I'm glad of it.

I've been told by some of my other neighbors during the past few months—the friendly ones, of course

—that those two former acquaintances are saying all sorts of things about me. For one thing, they delight in calling me a Northerner, which they consider a disdainful epithet, and they spread rumors that I've lost all my friends in Bastrop and that I'm so miserable that I'm begging my husband to resign from his position at the chemical plant so we can leave town.

If anybody's looking for an example of a closed society, you wouldn't have to go any farther than Bastrop to find it. I don't know if it's typical of the South, but it's sure plain hell to be surrounded by what's right here.

Some of the other gossip in Bastrop about me is that I have an immoral past and came South because I thought I could hide it here. One story is that I was somebody's mistress in Boston while I was going to college. And I was. And I'm proud of it. I've been my husband's only mistress since the first time I met him. That's something some of the gossiping matrons couldn't truthfully boast about—not if they knew their husbands as well as other people in town do.

Another thing I've heard is that I'm said to be partly Negro because I have dark skin and curly black hair and think I'm fooling everybody by trying to pass for a white person. What they don't know is that whatever I am suits me perfectly and I wouldn't want to be any different. I have no idea what they'll try to think of next to say about me, but it's sure to be the meanest thing they can think of.

There are only a few of us Northerners—as we're called—living in Bastrop right now and occasionally two or three of us will get together and talk about the gossip that's circulating about us in town. We have a few drinks, sympathize with each other, and then sometimes have a good cry together. Or a big laugh about it all. Either crying or laughing helps a lot. After that we can go home feeling like human beings again and not liked diseased untouchables.

But that kind of feeling never lasts long. After a few days there's sure to be some new despicable gossip in circulation. Not long ago it was said that I was going to try to desegregate our church by encouraging my maid, Kathy, and other Negroes to organize a sit-in demonstration during a Sunday morning service. I'd never thought of such a thing and had no such intention, even though I do think Negroes should have the right to join any church they wish and attend services like any other member.

Anyway, what happened was that the minister heard about it and he said it was up to the membership to decide if the church was to remain segregated or be desegregated. He said that instead of taking a standing vote during services, he had decided it would be better to circulate petitions among the members.

It was a foregone conclusion, as the minister knew, that very few people would sign a petition favoring integration of anything in Bastrop. Social and economic pressure against such a thing in a Southern town like this is too strong. But my husband and I signed in favor of it. And that did it. The whole thing was a trick, of course. It was all some people wanted to know when they saw our names on it and the petitions were immediately withdrawn before anybody else was asked to sign. The church is all-white—just as it's always been.

Ever since then I've been called a Negro-lover—or, as they delight in saying it, nigger-lover—civil rights agitator, communist organizer, and, of course, a Northerner. When my husband and I attend church services now on Sunday mornings, we get a very icy-cold reception. Our best friends speak to us, and the minister shakes hands as though performing a dis-tasteful duty, but you'd think by the way everybody else manages to look in some other direction that my husband and I had committed all the unpardonable sins in the book and were not only untouchable but also unlookables.

I supose the unpleasantness will wear away in time, if we live here long enough, but right now it's a terrible price to pay for having convictions and the courage to express them. It's worth it, though, to know that you still have the strength of character to stand up for what you believe in and not be cowed into submission to somebody else's prejudice.

There's no doubt that terrible things are happening to Negroes in many places in the South these days—including murder—but I can't imagine any place where there could possibly be more subtle hatred for the Negro than right here in Bastrop. Hatred has to be the word for it. Nothing else will express it. The Negroes know they are hated and they try to be careful not to make a move that might be displeasing to a white man and be an excuse for brutal retaliation.

I've never seen a white person spit at a Negro's face or deliberately run over a Negro child with his automobile, though I've heard that such things are done, but there are other things that reveal subtle hatred of Negroes.

Not long ago a new coin-operated washateria opened in town. It was so modern and well-equipped with the most up-to-date automatic washers and dryers that everybody wanted to use it. It had soft lighting and comfortable lounge chairs and vending machines for candy and drinks. The rest rooms were painted in pastel colors and lavishly mirrored and the whole place was more like a private club than anything else. As to be expected, there was a large sign posted at the entrance. FOR THE USE OF WHITES ONLY.

The owner of the washateria, seeing how successful it was, and being a good businessman, lost no time in finding a location for a second washateria for the exclusive use of Negroes. Identical modern equipment was installed—washers, dryers, lounge chairs, vending machines, and all the rest. The only difference was that there was no sign at the door of the newer place prohibiting its use by anybody.

Both washaterias were open day and night. The

second one had been operating for no more than a
week when late one night after the last Negro cus-
tomer had left, a group of white women drove up in
a car and waited outside until they were sure the
owner himself had gone home. Then, each woman
carrying two sacks of sand, they went inside, dumped
the sand into the machines, and inserted coins into
the slots. The machines started automatically. And
by the time they had completed their cycles every
washer and dryer in the place was damaged beyond
repair.

The owner locked the door the next day and has
never opened it since. Of course, the other washateria,
the one for whites only, remains in business as usual.

That's the way it is. And with that kind of hate
and spite in the atmosphere, it'll be a long time before anybody else will risk investing money in separate, but equal, washaterias for white and Negro.

I've been told that there's no longer a typical
Southern way of life. I'm not so sure about that. Being
a Northerner, now I'll have to be shown, instead of
being merely told, after what has happened here.

17

The time-scarred red-brick walls of the old Bogalusa city jail have been neatly plastered with cement and coated with gleaming white paint. The stately appearance of the building in the tree shaded plaza of the Bogalusa civic center might easily mislead a stranger in town to assume at first glance that it is either one of Louisiana's well-preserved ante-bellum mansions of historical importance or else a modern motel that had been expertly designed in neo-colonial architectural style.

Even the white-painted iron bars over the narrow windows of the jail look as if they had been placed there as a final ornamental touch to make sure that the outward appearance of the building would be architecturally authentic in every detail.

The Bogalusa jail looks much different on the outside in the ninteen-sixties, to be sure, but on the inside the dingy gray walls and the rusty iron cages and cell blocks look the same now as they did in the early nineteen-twenties.

I ought to know, because long ago I spent nine days and nights in one of the ceiling-high cages. I was there because I had no money, no job, and was four days and four dollars behind in rent at a Bogalusa walk-up hotel across the street from the railroad tracks.

It is likely that I would have spent ninety days and nights in the Bogalusa jail, and possibly even longer than that, if I had not been befriended by a fifty-year-old blue-black Negro trusty named Ramey Salty. Ramey said he might be too black-skinned to look like a real Gumbo, even if he did have straight hair and a French-English name, but that on the inside he felt just like an ordinary human being.

When I told Ramey how I came to be there, and without prospect of being released, he volunteered to help me get out at the risk of losing his own limited freedom. He said police were good people in some ways when they wanted to be, but that it was wrong of them to keep an eighteen-year-old white boy in jail because he owed somebody four dollars and not let him get back to college and finish his education.

Ramey Salty had been informally and unofficially sentenced to an indefinite term in jail for failing to stop making moonshine corn liquor with a homemade still in his shantytown house in the Negro quarter after several warnings by the police. He had admitted to the police that he had an uncontrollable weakness for making moonshine for himself and his friends and he himself had suggested that he be locked up in jail from dusk to dawn every night so he could keep out of trouble.

The only condition Ramey had proposed, and it was an acceptable one to the police, was that he would be permitted to leave jail during the daylight hours to work at his shoe-shining job in a barber shop near the railroad station. After two years it was still a satisfactory arrangement to both Ramey and the police.

As Ramey said about the arrangement, he was so well satisfied that he hoped he would never have to move out of jail and go back to shantytown in the Negro quarter. He said he had no wife to fuss at him for staying out at night and no house rent to pay every Saturday. There was running water and inside toilet in jail and he received two free meals of collards, fatback, and cornbread every day of the week. Besides, he made enough money shining shoes at the barber shop to pay for the clothes and tobacco he needed and to buy a pint of ready-made whisky whenever he pleased.

But there was even more to it than that. Ramey told me in confidence, after making me promise not to say a word about it to the police, that he had a secret reason for being so pleased about the arrangement he had made. His secret was that he was the only Negro in Bogalusa who could work and live in the segregated white part of the city and not have to go back to the Negro quarter to sleep at night. He said his ambition was to keep that distinction as long as he lived and then take the secret with him to his grave without white people in Bogalusa ever realizing that he had crossed their color line.

However, Ramey Salty was unhappy about my being in jail. He had told me the first time we talked about it that a colored man had to get used to being put in jail for little or no reason, but that he did not think it was right for the police to lock up a white boy who had been cheated out of his pay by a dishonest boss and left stranded in town without enough money to pay four dollars for room rent.

I had told Ramey about not having been paid after working for three nights selling magazine subscriptions to sawyers and papermakers in the Bogalusa lumber and pulpwood mills and that I owed four dollars at the hotel where I had been living. The owner of the walk-up hotel had locked me out of my room, taken my suitcase for non-payment of rent, and then called the police and told them that I was planning to leave town without paying what I owed him.

Ramey is dead now, more than forty years later, and I regret that I did not have an opportunity to see him again and tell him once more how grateful I was for his helping me get out of jail. Once I did send twenty dollars in a letter addressed to him in care of the Bogalusa jail, but I never knew if he received it.

It is good to know, though, that Ramey Salty never lost his dawn-to-dusk freedom from jail and did succeed in maintaining his residence in the segregated white section of Bogalusa. He continued to be a trusty until he died and was buried by the police in the Negro cemetery adjoining the Bogalusa Country Club. His grave is only a chip-shot over the fence from the restricted white-only golf course.

What had happened before I was befriended by Ramey was that spring had come early that year to South Carolina, where I was a student, and in the first week of April, without informing my parents or leaving a forwarding address, I had packed my suitcase and gone to New Orleans. There I soon found out that shucking oysters was a specialized job that required considerable training, that stevedoring was work that was done with seasoned muscles, and that dishwashing in a French Quarter café was monotonous and confining and something easily eliminated as even a temporary trade.

A want-ad in a newspaper offered exactly the kind of position I considered suitable. Three young men and two young women, no experience necessary, and college students preferred, were to be offered the opportunity to join an executive staff engaged in conducting a circulation campaign for a major magazine.

I was among the first applicants to knock on the crew manager's hotel door that morning in New

Orleans and become one of the five new members of the executive staff. At midnight all of us got on the train to Bogalusa, a sawmill and pulpwood town on the Pearl River in Southeast Louisiana, and we were given free copies of the magazine to look at along the way. We arrived at six o'clock the next morning and got rooms on the second floor of the walk-up hotel near the railroad station.

The crew manager, a blond young man who appeared to be about twenty-seven or twenty-eight and who carried a very small suitcase for what he had said would be a month of travel, told us that it was against the company policy to advance money for meals and other personal expenses. However, he promised us that the circulation campaign would begin promptly at seven o'clock that evening when the night shifts went to work at the mills and that we would begin earning commissions right away.

While sitting at the window of my room in the hotel and waiting for night to come so I could make some money for a meal, I saw the crew manager take the two girls to a café across the street for breakfast. After a while the three of them came back to the room next to mine, locked the door, and stayed there until late in the afternoon. Just before dark, after several hours of squeaking bedsprings, loud giggling, and the slam-bang of upset chairs, they left the room and went across the street again for an early dinner.

That night while the two girls entertained the shift

superintendent in his office, we went through the
mill selling dollar-a-year subscriptions to the magazine devoted to hunting, fishing, diagrams of home
hobbies for men, and pictures of girls posing as
artists' models. The crew manager, right behind us,
collected the subscription orders and the money after
each sale. When we finished at midnight, he tore up
all the subscriptions we had sold to Negroes, saying
most of them could not read and none of them had
any business looking at pictures of naked white girls,
and told us that we would be paid the commissions
we had earned—including the sales to Negroes—after
he had made up his accounts in a day or two.

After three nights of the circulation campaign, and
still not having settled with us, the crew manager
and the two girls disappeared. The other two salesmen had enough money of their own to pay their
hotel bills and buy train tickets back to New Orleans.
All I had was about forty cents in nickels and dimes.

I had been in the Bogalusa jail for two days and
nights when Ramey Salty said one of the jailers had
told him that I would probably be charged with failure to pay the four-dollar hotel bill and be given a
three-month sentence. Ramey said he had asked the
jailers to let him pay the four dollars for me but that
they would not accept the money from him. He was
warned that he would get into serious trouble himself and might even lose the privilege of living there
if he did not stop trying to help me get out of jail.

On the third day at sundown when Ramey came

back from the barber shop, he stopped at my cell and gave me a ham-and-cheese sandwich he had smuggled past the jailers by hiding it inside his shirt. When I saw him take out the sandwich, it was a startling reminder of the time I took pork chops to Roy at the chain-gang stockade in Georgia.

While I was eating the sandwich, Ramey, watching me with a pleased smile covering his wrinkled dark face, said it was the closest thing to home-cooking he could smuggle into jail. For the past three days I had eaten very little of the jail meal of boiled collards, boiled fatback, and soggy cornbread handed twice a day to each prisoner—white and Negro alike —in a quart-size tin bucket.

After I had thanked Ramey for the sandwich, he went to his cell and sat down on the bunk. He was too far away for me to be able to see what he was doing, but presently he left his cell, which the jailers never bothered to lock, and came back to my cell with his hand pressing against something else inside his shirt. Coming close to the bars, he handed me a sheet of paper, an envelope, and the stub of a pencil he had collected. I could see some of the other prisoners watching us through the bars of their cells, but none of them said anything.

Whispering to me in order to keep the jailer in the front room from hearing him and becoming suspicious, Ramey told me what he wanted me to do. He said he knew I had parents or relatives somewhere and that he was sure I would be kept in jail for the next three months or even longer if I did not write to somebody who would be able to help me get released. He told me that it would do no good at all to give the jailers a letter to mail, because he had seen them open letters other prisoners had written and then, after reading the letters, throw them into the wastebasket.

The lights in the cell room had been turned off for the night and it would be morning before I could see well enough to write a letter. And by then Ramey would have left for the day and be unable to mail the letter for me. He did not want to waste a whole day getting my letter into the mail, and he told me to write it as soon as there was enough light in the morning. Then I was to climb to the top of the cell and look out the window for a small colored boy who would be playing in the weeds behind the jail.

Ramey said all I had to do then was to whistle to the boy and drop the letter through the bars. He said the boy would take the letter to him at the barber shop and then he would take care of everything else after that.

I asked Ramey why he was trying to help me the way he was doing since there were ten or twelve of us in jail and he offered no help to the others. He said everybody else ought to be kept where they were, because they had been jailed for stealing or knifing or doing something else just as bad, and that the only reason I was there was because I had been cheated and could not pay the four dollars I owed.

That was when I told him about some other Negroes I had known—Bisco in Georgia and Sonny in Tennessee and Troy in Mississippi—and Ramey said he believed in friendship among the races and wished there could be more of it.

That was when he asked if I had seen Bisco recently. After telling him that I had not seen Bisco since that time when I wanted to spend the night in his house, I said that I did not know if he would still be in Middle Georgia or if he had moved away, but that I hoped to find him sometime wherever he was. Ramey said that he was going to be sure to remember the name but that he hoped he would never see Bisco in the Bogalusa jail.

When Ramey came back to the jailhouse at his usual time at the end of the day, he told me that the letter I had dropped through the window that morning had been stamped and mailed and that he was sure something good would happen within a few days. After a while he admitted that something had gone wrong in the beginning but that everything had worked out all right in the end. What had happened was that the colored boy who took my letter was not the one Ramey had sent. However, he had found out who the boy was and got the letter back and then had mailed it himself.

In the afternoon of the fifth day after Ramey had mailed the letter, one of the jailers unlocked my cell door and told me I was free to leave. I had written the letter to my father in Georgia and I expected to see him waiting for me. Instead, the secretary of the Bogalusa YMCA introduced himself and said that my father had telegraphed money for the hotel bill and a train ticket to Atlanta.

When we got to the YMCA, I took a shower, changed clothes—the secretary had already paid the four-dollar hotel bill and got my suitcase—and then I ate a meal of something other than collards, fat-back, and cornbread for the first time in nine days.

On the way to the railroad station to take the train to Birmingham, and from there to Atlanta, I told the secretary I wanted to stop at the barber shop and see Ramey Salty before I left Bogalusa and thank him for all he had done for me. While I was eating dinner at the YMCA, I had told the secretary that Ramey urged me to write the letter and then mailed it for me.

The secretary shook his head emphatically and said it would be better if I left town without seeing Ramey. Then he told me that the police were trying to find out how I had smuggled a letter out of jail and that they suspected Ramey of having mailed it for me. He said Bogalusa was a small town and that if I were seen talking to Ramey at the barber shop, the police would be certain to find out about it and would probably take away his privileges. I knew that if that happened he would have to leave jail and go back to the Negro quarter to live.

I left Bogalusa without seeing Ramey Salty again. Knowing how much he wanted to live on the white side of town, I was sure thereafter that it was a favor Ramey would appreciate more than any other thing I could have done for him.

18

There are not many things in modern times that have had the endurance and tenacity to span fifty years without perceptible change. But, as if to prove that some things do resist mutation, the landscape surrounding an early homeplace in Coweta County in Middle Georgia can still present a familiar appearance even after a half-century.

The red clay hills are undoubtedly more deeply eroded and gully-washed, the sky-line of jagged pines probably juts higher against the horizon, the stark spires of crumbling brick chimneys have become melancholy monuments to homes burned to ashes, briar thickets and clumps of beggar-lice have been quick to claim possession of abandoned cotton fields, and the gaunt granite gravestones in the cemetery have taken on the somber gray moss of age and oblivion.

Just the same, here and now, and unyielding to time, meandering minnow-rippled creeks continue to run their age-old courses, the cut-bank clay is still bright red in color, sassafras saplings sprout bountifully in the hedgerows, crows caw mournfully in the corn fields, and, as always, the crooked dirt roads inevitably lead to back-country isolation and loneliness.

Once, and not so long ago in history, either, this was Indian country—the hunting grounds of the Cherokees, the Chocktaws, and the Creeks. Then for a century and longer it has been the home of the white landowner, the sharecropper, and the poor buckra, and, likewise, a place of living for the mulatto, quadroon, and octoroon descendants of the Geechee Negroes who migrated to the Middle Georgia uplands from the lowland plantations after freedom from slavery.

This buckshot soil and wiregrass land between the rock-ledged Piedmont in the north and the fertile earth in the south has sustained life for generations but it has failed to enrich it. It is the nature of such medial land to ensnare the unwary with generous promises in the spring and then fail to fulfill its pledges in the autumn. Nevertheless, during all this time, people with valiant hope remain and wait for a better year to come.

Bisco's chink-log birthplace had disappeared from sight and without even a chimney brick remaining to show for it. The bucket-windlass well had been filled with the brick and rubble of the house and there were not even stumps left of the leafy chinaberry trees. Together with the cotton field and the black-berry thicket, all the land had been contoured and seeded and fenced for a cattle pasture.

What was left of my own birthplace by the side of the road was merely a rubble of crumbled chimney brick. The ownership of the land had changed several times during the past decades and very few people remained who had knowledge or recollection of anyone, white or Negro, who had lived in the neighborhood so long ago. Some of the previous landowners and storekeepers of the community had moved to nearby towns or to adjoining counties and others were buried under the oak trees in the white cemetery at the crossroads.

Also, many Negroes had left Coweta County in the nineteen-twenties to work in Chicago, Detroit, and Philadelphia and had remained there to live. Later, others had gone to Atlanta and Washington to attend school or to seek jobs and had never returned.

And so at first, no one could be found who recognized the name Bisco, or even Nabisco or Frisco or Brisco, although there were a few Negroes on surrounding farms who were between sixty and eighty years old and had lived in the community all their lives.

A deeply wrinkled Negro woman, white haired and past seventy, was living alone in a one-room cabin at the end of a long path through a cotton field. Geechee-mulatto in coloring and stoop-backed after a lifetime of washing clothes and picking cotton, she said that she had always lived in the neighborhood and thought she knew everybody during that time who had been born and raised within three or four miles.

If I only knowed his last name, or his daddy's name, she said, I might could maybe put something enough together to figure out just who he's apt to be and where to find him if he's still alive and around here somewhere. Everybody colored I speak to goes to preaching at the China Grove African Church— leastways they go to preaching there when they get jobbed hard about it or had a bad nightmare about hell-fire and hurry to the church to save their souls.

Nobody can't keep from knowing folks if you make a habit of going to preaching at the church all the time like I do. I've been a sister in the church a good part of all my life and that's the best way to remember folks by name and looks and the promises they make to support the preacher. That's because a good sister has to help the deacons keep after the sinners and backsliders and pester them to reach down deep and put in some money so the preacher'll have a little ready cash to live on.

It just aint right to have to stand by and see a hard-up preacher get out in the field in the hot sun every day but Sunday and grow cotton and corn for a living like ordinary folks has to do.

And it don't look no better to go by and see a

preacher slopping hogs and feeding chickens for his whole living, neither. But it looks like they had to do a little of that. None of them never gets enough cash money from the church collections to live on. Maybe somewhere else the preachers do, but not around here they don't.

What I was aiming to say was that who you're talking about might come back to mind if I could just shut my eyes and see what he looked like sitting in a pew at the church or standing up singing. If I had that much of a lead, then I'd be sure to remember him, because he'd be bound to be somebody I used to have to track down in the field or follow home after the preaching to argue with him about paying a little more cash money to help keep the preacher and his family going.

When folks don't pay the preacher enough for him to get by on without having to do ordinary work on the side, the first thing you know he's going to pick up and go off to some other place in a different part of the country where he can make a fresh new start all over again and get paid real cash money for praying and preaching. There's been preachers right here at the China Grove African Church who stayed only two or three months or so and then picked up and left just for that reason and I couldn't blame them none at all.

I always worked hard and done my best to collect money for the preachers. But the way it's now the young folks around here has got the habit of claiming they don't have no spare money to hand out like that. That's not exactly a sinful lie, neither. It's mostly the truth when they say they don't have no spare money.

I know about that. The money's all gone to pay for something before it gets to be spare. Nowadays when somebody gets hold of some money, they spend it as fast as they can. What don't go to put down on the charges at the stores they sign up for, they spend to buy gas for their old car and drive down the road to Luthersville or up to Newnan to visit and have a good time.

Now, when you come right down to it, I just can't get my mind to remember nobody named Bisco or nothing like that. But I'm downright sure he wasn't no preacher. There's never been a preacher around here with a name like that.

A mile farther down the narrow dirt road, a gray-haired tobacco-brown Negro who appeared to be at least seventy years old was sitting on a bench close to the sunny side of the two-room tenant house. He was wearing a tattered gray sweater, patched over-alls, mud-caked shoes, and a shapeless black-felt winter hat. At the rear of the house, his wife was taking clothes from an iron washpot and hanging them on the garden fence. Wrapped in a colorful. shawl, but shivering in the cool spring air, she too was elderly and her skin coloring was a faded shade of brown.

Surrounding the weather-gray wooden house were several acres of sharecropping cotton land. Last year's stunted brown cotton stalks were still standing in the field as if to be a forewarning of another year's meager crop to come from the crusty buckshot soil.

I seem to recollect a little bit about who you're talking about, he said. I can't remember nothing about what his whole true name was, besides Bisco and Nabisco or something like that, but I used to live over near there where you said the house was where he lived used to be. I used to see his daddy, too, but his daddy died a long time ago. After his daddy died, that old house just rotted away and fell down and the white man bulldozed it away to get rid of it for his cattle pasture. I don't know exactly where his mammy went after that. I reckon she moved away to town somewhere.

Anyhow. The white man who owned the land over there got rid of what was left of that old house and then plowed right through the yard and where the house was when he got ready to turn all his land to pasturing for some cows. That was while a big war was going on. That boy went away to the war and stayed somewhere a long time. Then when he came back, he went to work for wages at a sawmill not far from here. Then it seems to me like he got in some kind of trouble talking too much and went away again somewhere for a while.

I just can't think exactly what that boy's trouble was about—except maybe talking back to a white man out of turn. Anyhow. He went up North some-where, I heard, and stayed up there till he got word his mammy died. She'd already been brought back here from town and buried in the China Grove ceme-tery by the time he got here, but he bought a tomb-stone and set it on her grave.

I know exactly where that tombstone's at in the cemetery and I could show it to you if I had me a way to get there. My old legs aint what they used to be. I has a hard time following the plow out there in the field and that makes me have to sit down and rest a lot when I ought to keep on plowing but can't.

I still don't remember what that boy's trouble was at the sawmill, except talking. He didn't steal nothing and he didn't cut nobody and he didn't try to fight nobody. There wasn't no shooting or knifing, like it's sometimes claimed by the white folks when a colored gets in trouble. And I'm positive it wasn't nothing about molesting a white woman, neither. It was all done talking too much out of turn to a white man. That's nearly always the way trouble gets started for the colored.

Anyhow. Now I seem to remember more about it when I keep on thinking about it. Something about his wages. He said his pay was shorted. That's what it was. He claimed he got short paid working over-time at the sawmill on a Saturday all day long and only got paid half-day regular wages. I don't know the right about it. Anyhow. The white boss said he wasn't going to pay him nothing more at all and told

Bisco to shut his mouth about it or else get clear out of the country in a hurry. That Bisco was a big strong man then, but he had sense enough to walk off and not start a fight with the white boss. That's when he left here and went up North somewhere, I reckon. Then like I said, he heard about his mammy being dead and he came back and put up that tombstone on her grave in the China Grove cemetery. He was good to his old mammy—both when she was alive and dead. That's the kind of man Bisco was.

The more I sit here and think about it now, more of it comes back to mind. Bisco settled down in Coweta County after that and went to sharecropping and got married and had some children. That wife he married was a perky young one. Maybe no more than fourteen or fifteen at the time and mighty good looking. She wasn't a real black girl. She was a heap lighter in color than some white folks I've seen. That Bisco wasn't no black boy, neither. He was real tan and more so than me.

Anyhow. Some white folks who moved here from somewhere else and bought some farm land got to talking about how his wife was too light-colored even for a Geechee and said Bisco married a white woman from the North and was trying to pass her off for colored so he could live with her. I never did know the truth about that and made it no business of mine to find out. Anyhow. These white folks said they wouldn't stand for no colored man living with no white woman and getting in the bed with her and they told him to get shed of her or else get out of the country himself. White or colored, I don't care which, nobody wants to get shed of his wife if she suits him and's the kind he wants to keep. Anyhow. Bisco said he wasn't going to do nothing about it like he was told.

Some good white folks sided with Bisco and said they didn't think it was right to make him get shed of his wife. But those other kind of white folks who started the trouble was the rich new people who owned a heap of the land and they stirred up some of the poor buckras to nightride.

I didn't think none of the whites who'd always lived around here would go against our people like that, but some of them did. That's when the night-riders went to Bisco's house one night and told him he had to sunrise the next morning to get clear out of Coweta County and never come back again as long as he lived.

Anyhow. Everybody knows what some white men'll do when they get a grudge against the colored and talk like that. If they go nightriding, they can make a colored disappear and you never see him again unless someday you happen to come across of what's left of him in a swamp somewhere. Anyhow. Bisco went ahead and done what I'd done. He loaded up his automobile with belongings and put his wife and children in it and drove off to somewhere long before sunrise.

And he aint been back since, neither. I've heard it

said he went over to Alabama or Mississippi, and maybe even more far off than that somewhere. I don't blame him none for going off as far as he could get from here. A colored never has no chance once the nightriders come around and take out a grudge on him for being colored. If they don't beat the life out of him to start with, they're just as apt to stuff pure cement down his throat and then weight him down with scrap iron in a swamp somewhere. I sure was glad Bisco got away alive.

Some folks say they've got letters in the mail from Bisco's wife and she says they're doing fine where they're at. I still don't know if it's Alabama or Mississippi or somewhere else. But every time I heard about it, it made me feel real good, because everybody knows what the nightriders would've done if he'd stayed here and kept his wife and not left like they told him to.

Anyhow. I'm none too pleased staying here myself where those same nightriding white men live all around and the colored still here about. They haven't bothered nobody lately but that don't mean they won't if they take a notion. Anyhow. I keep my mouth shut tight when I'm around one of them. I'm too old now for me to pick up and make a move like Bisco done. I wouldn't even know which way to go off somewhere to.

19

Some roads lead out of the Deep South, some go around in inconsequential circles, others come to a dead end at the brink of sinister swamps, and a few roads go all the way to New Orleans.

A person who takes one of the roads to New Orleans and goes there after time spent in the countryside and in other cities of the Southern states is likely to get the impression that New Orleans is a little bit of everything the Old South was in the past and some of what the New South is now. Most of all, however, he is likely to get the immediate impression that New Orleans has the fortune to be unique among all Southern cities.

After the impression will come considerable evidence that the uniqueness of New Orleans is durable and memorable and incontestable. The humid climate of the city and its deep-water port are duplicated around the world. The conglomeration of modern architecture and ancient housing in New Orleans is similar to that of many American cities. But nowhere in the Deep South, or anywhere else in the United States, is there a comparable compound of people whose origins are French, Spanish, Italian, German, English, Scottish, Irish, Scandinavian, Mexican, Cuban, African, Indian, Cajun, Creole, and Gumbo.

This unique admixture of nearly a million people of the world has produced a New Orleans family of man that could be duplicated elsewhere only in the imagination of an anthropologist.

As the result of generations of racial commingling and assimilation, New Orleans is the one place in Bisco Country where social conflict has the best opportunity of being adjudged by intelligence and sympathy rather than by the agony of physical force and violence. New Orleans has had its share of racial disturbances in the past and, like other American cities in the Racial Sixties, it will be subjected to more in the future. Nevertheless, because of the sympathy and sophistication of its population, a mutually satisfactory adjustment of social and civil rights is likely to be achieved with more ease and quickness in New Orleans than elsewhere in the United States.

It has been the progressive blending of the city's heterogeneous population for more than two centuries that accounts for the noticeable contrast between the human compatibility and cosmopolitanism of New Orleans and, differing so distinctly, the innumerable pockets of racial conflict and disparity in the hinterland beginning at its own city limits and extending all the way from Louisiana to South Carolina.

Beyond the city limits of New Orleans and throughout the hinterland there is fear and belligerency among Negroes and, most basic of all, cautious mistrust and suspicion of the white man and his motives. There is good reason for being mistrustful of the white man anywhere in Bisco Country, as Negroes have learned during years of painful experience, and parents have passed the warning along to their children. The fear has been generated over the years by threats and intimidation, by beatings and killings, and mistrust is a logical defense against injury.

The older generation of Negroes have been cowed by fear and their only refuge is in mistrust. Among the younger generation, belligerency takes the form of active protests and demonstrations and, in the extreme, physical retaliation with fists and sticks and stones.

In any form, this contention is a revolutionary step beyond fear and mistrust. Those who are actively belligerent are the new-age Negroes of the Racial Sixties who, unlike their parents and grandparents, have been freed from fear by education and visions of equality.

In the past, poverty and its miseries were described

by romanticists—and by theorists—as being a sympathetic bond between underprivileged whites and Negroes. Such a common bond did not exist in actual life in the Deep South and it still has no basis of fact. What actually happened was that in a showdown between the two, it was customary for the white-skin man to receive favored treatment from landlord and politician at the expense of the black-skin man. This was a traditional bribe paid to the poor-white to help keep the Negro in economic bondage and political subjection. Consequently, it was inevitable that Negroes would eventually become suspicious of the motives of the whole white race.

The difference between being white-poor and Negro-poor in such an environment is that the former has had freedom of opportunity and movement and the latter has been a prisoner of discrimination and injustice. Long after civil rights legislation and conscientious efforts to enforce the law, this racial zoning in Bisco Country will continue to be as conspicuous as the distinct lines of demarcation between residential and commercial zoning of real estate in any American city.

This is why poverty in Bisco Country did not begin merely because there was insufficient money for an individual to buy adequate food and clothing for his family. Poverty actually began when the human spirit of the Negro American was impoverished by the denial of the rights of citizenship. Urban or rural in environment, physical hunger and distress might be endured by a man of any race with little alleviation, but withholding the Negro's freedom and equality while granting it to others who happened to have been born with white skin was more tragic in its psychological consequences than material poverty.

The inevitable human reaction to this injustice was the cause of the rebellion of the Racial Sixties.

During the progress of the Negro rebellion, no community in the Deep South will be privileged to have immunity from violence in the contest between equality and superiority. On one side are willful men who take pride and comfort in racial hate and they are not about to give up life-long prejudice and accept equality with Negroes without a struggle. On the other side are Negroes whose long-promised sweet-by-and-by can no longer be denied or postponed. In another age, after prejudice has been buried with the last survivor of Old South traditions, such a controversy is not likely to exist and certainly not tolerated for long.

However, this being the nineteen-sixties, and an immediacy, the younger generation of whites and Negroes in New Orleans are not waiting for the future but are striving to reach truce and agreement now for the purpose of alleviating the aggravations that lead to conflict and riot. If such efforts are successful, New Orleans will have additional pride in its uniqueness.

In contrast to the contemporary sophistication of

New Orleans and the racial blending of its population—as well as a reminder of the deep-seated traditions of its hinterland—it would be well to look back
into the past and to recall the era of the old-time
darky when he was groveling in the dust and then
trotting off in feigned cheerful obedience to the white
master's command.

On a Deep South plantation even as recently as a
generation ago he was an elderly Gullah or Geechee
or Guinea or Gumbo, white-haired and stoop-shoul-
dered, who was dressed in ragged clothing and had
been trained from youth by lash or deprivation to
live in constant fear of displeasing the whole white
race. And, if he were a good darky, he received the
favor of being called Uncle.

Because of his advanced age and failing health, he
was no longer useful as a fieldhand. However, assumed to be senile, and therefore as trustworthy and
harmless as a eunuch in the proximity of white
women, his being permitted to be yardboy and buffoon was his ultimate reward for a lifetime of labor
in the fields.

Knowing by years of experience what was required
of him, he listened to orders, hat in hand, with abject
humility. When dismissed, he backed away from the
white master to a respectful distance before daring
to turn around and go off to his chore. His day began
at dawn when he went to the back porch of the
master's mansion to wait patiently for the first command of the morning. His day ended when he saw

the last light in the big house turned off at midnight or later. His pay was left-over food from the kitchen, the shelter of a barnyard crib, and occasional gifts of discarded clothing.

In addition to his many regularly prescribed daily chores, such as saddling a horse, raking leaves, splitting firewood, plucking a chicken, butchering a hog, hoeing the garden, sweeping the porches, and cleaning the backhouse privy, the elderly yardboy and buffoon was often required to obey whimsical commands to perform antics on Sunday afternoons and holidays for the amusement of the master and his guests.

There were times when Uncle Ned—or Uncle Pete or Uncle Jack—would be told to climb a tree in the front yard and to sit there on a limb until he saw a buzzard fly overhead. Sometimes he would be told to run around in circles and howl like a hound treeing a possum. He could be ordered to get down on his knees and pray aloud for rain to fall on all the cornfields in the county without a drop of water falling on cottonfields. He might be told to make up words for a song, and to sing it as loudly as he could about a high-yellow girl begging a white man to chase her into the woods. Many of these musical laments and mournful prayers with improvised lyrics lived in memory to become the enduring folk songs of the South.

Now and then there were Sunday afternoon occasions—but always after the minister and his wife and

children had finished eating midday dinner and had
gone home—when the men left the women on the
front porch or in the parlor and went down to the
barn.

Going-to-the-barn was a special event for the men
and usually it was an occasion that could be antici-
pated after hearing a casual hint several days in
advance. There the men could drink bourbon from
bottles and watch an exhibition on the corn-husking
floor that the elderly Negro had been ordered to
arrange. It was his duty at a time like that to use a
shotgun if necessary to bring a young buck and a
girl to the barn from the Negro quarter to strip naked
and perform whatever sexually inciting acts the men
said they wanted to see. Afterward, the older white
men went back to the house and the younger ones
could stay in the barn and take turns mounting the
girl on the corn-husking floor. At a time like that, a
white man had no qualms about crossing the color
line with a Negro girl. In fact, on remote plantations
it was often a customary ritual to celebrate achievement of Southern manhood.

It is not likely that the Old South plantation custom of going-to-the-barn is to be found anywhere in
Bisco Country in the nineteen-sixties. However, whenever there is a portrayal of such a custom, it was probably conceived in satire by a little theatre group of
composers, lyricists, singers, and musicians as an up-
dated folk song called "Happy Integration—You-All,"
and reminiscent of the tune to "Massa's in the Cold

Cold Ground." And if the performance took place in New Orleans, in particular, there surely would be recognizable overtones of traditionally classic Negro blues and jazz in every rendition.

The search for Bisco has led to the rhythmic din of blues and jazz of New Orleans. There is no sound of a funeral dirge in the narrow streets behind the levee and that is to be taken as a good omen that he can yet be found.

The tempestuous music seems to be saying that Bisco is still somewhere in his native land—somewhere in Bisco Country—with tales of a lifetime of joy and sorrow as a Negro American.